M000044239

rebel lives **helen keller** rebel lives **helen keller** rebel lives

**rebel lives**, a fresh new series of inexpensive, accessible and provocative books unearthing the rebel histories of some familiar figures and introducing some lesser-known rebels

**rebel lives**, selections of writings by and about remarkable women and men whose radicalism has been concealed or forgotten. Edited and introduced by activists and researchers around the world, the series presents stirring accounts of race, class and gender rebellion

**rebel lives**, does not seek to canonize its subjects as perfect political models, visionaries or martyrs but to make available the ideas and stories of imperfect revolutionary human beings to a new generation of readers and aspiring rebels

# helen keller

edited by John Davis

**Ocean Press**
Melbourne ■ New York
www.oceanbooks.com.au

Cover design by Sean Walsh and Meaghan Barbuto

ISBN 1-876175-60-5

Library of Congress Catalog Card No: 2003102870

First Printed in Australia 2003

**Published by Ocean Press**

**Australia:**    GPO Box 3279, Melbourne, Victoria 3001, Australia
           Fax: (61-3) 9329 5040 Tel: (61-3) 9326 4280
           E-mail: info@oceanbooks.com.au

**USA:**        PO Box 1186, Old Chelsea Stn., New York, NY 10113-1186, USA
           Tel: (718) 246-4160

**Ocean Press Distributors:**

*United States and Canada:* **Consortium Book Sales and Distribution**
           1045 Westgate Drive, Suite 90, Saint Paul, MN 55114-1065, USA
           Tel: 1-800-283-3572

*Britain and Europe:* **Global Book Marketing**
           38 King Street, London, WC2E 8JT, UK

*Australia and New Zealand:* **Palgrave Macmillan**
           627 Chapel Street, South Yarra, Victoria, 3141, Australia
           E-mail: customer.service@macmillan.com.au

*Cuba and Latin America*: **Ocean Press**
           Calle 21 #406, Vedado, Havana, Cuba

**www.oceanbooks.com.au**

# contents

# introduction

Helen Keller is best known as a deaf and blind girl who learned to communicate by touch. According to orthodox biographies she was an unruly child who, in 1888, at the age of eight, was "tamed" by a saint-like teacher, Anne Sullivan, who taught her manners and the manual alphabet.

The popular image of Keller suspends her in adolescence — a nice, brave, patient girl who's sightless eyes stare placidly into space as she fingers a Braille manuscript.

But what was she reading?

Keller attended the prestigious Radcliffe College, thanks in part to a fund set up by Mark Twain to fund her education. As a university student she became radicalized through her research on the social and economic causes of blindness. Noting her growing interest in social and political issues, Anne Sullivan recommended H.G. Wells's *New Worlds For Old*, for its "imaginative quality" and "electric style," although Sullivan herself did not agree with Wells' socialism. Keller found the book a revelation.

Sullivan's husband, John Macy, was a socialist intellectual with an extensive library of political books that Keller consumed voraciously. By her late 20s she was reading socialist periodicals in German Braille and a friend came three times a week to spell books on Marxist economics into her hand, letter by letter.

The selection of speeches, essays and articles in this book, largely written by Keller herself, reveal a woman of fierce intellect, driven by the strength of her political convictions to champion the most radical of causes at a time when to be a left radical was to risk vilification and imprisonment.

Despite vitriolic and insulting attacks in the press Keller became a passionate advocate for working people and joined the U.S. Socialist Party in 1909 and the Industrial Workers of the World (IWW) soon after. She campaigned against World War I, advocated reproductive rights and votes for women and supported Lenin, the Bolsheviks and the Russian Revolution. The FBI kept her under surveillance for most of her adult life.

To those who ascribed her political "mistakes" to disability she gave as good as she got:

> If I cannot see the fire at the end of their cigarettes, neither can they thread a needle in the dark. All I ask, gentlemen, is a fair field and no favor. I have entered the fight against preparedness [for U.S. entry into World War I] and against the economic system under which we live. It is to be a fight to the finish and I ask no quarter.

A search for materials on the life and work of Helen Keller yields hundreds of essays, texts and dedications, but the story contained in most is disturbingly homogenous; a young Helen Keller overcomes deafness and blindness and learns to communicate. Some sources make vague references to her being a great humanitarian, or a campaigner for the rights of the deaf and blind, but few mention her "rebel years" in the first two decades of the 20th century.

This book can provide a starting point for those interested in Helen Keller as a political activist and thinker. Like other books in the *Rebel Lives* series, it is designed to make Keller's own words available to readers for whom rebel histories have, to some degree, been concealed or overlooked. What has been written about Keller is not wholly inaccurate or fabricated, but key parts of her life and work have been excised. In the radical education journal *Rethinking Schools* Ruth Hubbard reviewed six popular children's books on Keller's life. The best-selling children's book, *A Girl Named Helen Keller*, by Lundell, is typical in its over-emphasis on Keller's childhood and its trite summary of her adult life:

> In her life, Helen wrote five books. She traveled many places. She met kings and presidents. She spoke to groups of people around the world. Most of the work she did was to help people who were blind or deaf. She was a warm and caring person. People loved her in return. The life of Helen Keller brought hope to many.

She spoke to groups of people around the world but what, asks Hubbard, did Keller actually say to them? Lundell's account does not hint that she said things like:

> The future of America rests on the backs of 80 million working-men and women and their children. We are facing a grave crisis in our national life. The few who profit from the labor of the masses want to organize the workers into an army which will protect the interests of the capitalists. You are urged to add to the heavy burdens you already bear the burden of a larger army and many additional warships. It is in your power to refuse to carry the artillery... You do not need to make a great noise about it. With the silence and dignity of creators you can end wars and the system of selfishness and exploitation that causes wars. All you need to do to bring about this stupendous revolution is to straighten up and fold your arms.

Hubbard concludes that the mythical Helen Keller, "angelic, sexless, deafblind woman smelling a rose as she holds a Braille book on her lap," has been constructed primarily to impart "a politically conservative moral lesson, one that stresses the ability of the individual to overcome personal adversity in a fair world. The lesson we are meant to learn seems to be: 'Society is fine the way it is. Look at Helen Keller! Even though she was deaf and blind, she worked hard — with a smile on her face — and overcame her disabilities.' "

Helen Keller would not have approved of this myth making. The adult Keller recognized that class privilege (her father was a prosperous newspaper editor who could afford to consult Alexander Graham Bell regarding his daughter's disabilities, and she was also supported financially by benefactors such as the railway magnate Andrew Carnegie) had provided her with opportunities not available to most. "I owed my success partly to the advantages of my birth and environment," she said. "I have learned that the power to rise is not within the reach of everyone."

## part one: Disability and Class

The first of Keller's writings reproduced here is also chronologically the earliest in the anthology. *I Must Speak* (1901) was published in the *Ladies' Home Journal* when Keller was 21 and in her second year at the prestigious Radcliffe College.

In this article Keller the rebel is clearly struggling to emerge from the ladylike conventions of her privileged upbringing, Radcliffe and the *Ladies' Home Journal*. She dares to write, albeit demurely, of venereal disease (linked to ophthalmia neonatorum) and she advocates a scientific approach to the causation and prevention of disability and rejects the religious acceptance of "blind eyes and deaf ears... as we accept the havoc of tornadoes and deluges."

Ten years later in *Social Causes of Blindness* (1911) and *The Unemployed* (1911) she makes no apology for her class-based analysis of deafness and blindness and advocates openly for the deaf and blind to align themselves with the working class in a joint struggle for liberation. *The Unemployed* was first published in *Ziegler Magazine for the Blind,* and was an attempt by Keller to educate and radicalize the working blind, a group traditionally ignored by most political organizations. In it she reiterates that it was her "investigation into blindness [that] led me into the industrial world."

Keller practiced what she preached. Her 1912 message *To the Strikers at Little Falls, New York* is just one of many such messages she wrote to workers on picket lines around the United States. It was written as a response to the violent suppression of a textile workers' strike. Later Keller identified the Little Falls strike as a turning point in the development of her ideas and the event that triggered her decision to join the IWW.

As an intellectual Keller rarely had the opportunity to take industrial action herself, but in 1919 she participated in a strike called by Actors Equity at a New York theater where she was appearing a silent film about her life, *Deliverance*. The actors at the theater were in dispute with management regarding their wages and Keller joined their picket line and spoke at their strike meetings. She declared that she would "rather have the film fail than aid the managers in their contest with the players." (*Call*, 1919)

The final two pieces in Part One, *The Underprivileged* (1931) and *Comments to the House Committee on Labor* (1944) are included here because they indicate that even in her later, more politically muted, years Keller retained a class perspective in her disability rights work.

## part two: Socialism

Part Two opens with Keller's fiery declaration of her political position. *How I Became a Socialist* (1912), published in the U.S. Socialist Party daily, the *Call,* was written when Keller's involvement with the Socialist Party was at its peak. Here Keller maps out the intellectual process that convinced her of socialism, writing, "It is no easy and rapid thing to absorb through one's fingers a book of 50,000 words on economics. But it is a pleasure, and

one which I will enjoy repeatedly until I have made myself acquainted with all the socialist authors." The article was the first widely
read declaration of her beliefs. Up to that point she had limited
herself to a few letters and sporadic conversations with reporters.

How I Became a Socialist is also a feisty response to an
attack by the editor of the Brooklyn Eagle, a Mr. McKelway, who
had written that Keller's political "mistakes" were a result of the
"manifest limitations of her development." McKelway is put firmly
in his place: "I can read all the socialist books I have time for in
English, German and French," writes an irate Keller. "If [McKelway]
should read some of them, he might be a wiser man and make a
better newspaper."

Keller was a member of the Socialist Party from 1908. By
1916 she had shifted her primary allegiance to the more industrially focused IWW. Although the Socialist Party had been
involved in the 1905 formation of the IWW (originally conceived
as an alternative union to the conservative union federation of the
time) and many activists, including Keller, were members of both
organizations, by 1916 the two had diverged. The IWW counter-
posed their industrial direct action tactics to the Socialist Party's
"political" participation in elections.

The IWW was the most radical and militant workers' organization of the day. In the 1910s and 1920s colorful IWW figures
such as "Big Bill" Haywood, Mother Jones, Joe Hill and Elizabeth
Gurley Flynn were identified with many fierce industrial battles
that involved thousands of the poorest paid workers, including
black workers, immigrants and women.

Keller's dissatisfaction with the primarily electoral activity of
the Socialist Party and her growing preference for industrial direct
action tactics are evident from as early as 1911, but it wasn't
until the New York Tribune ran an interview with Keller entitled
Why I Became an IWW (1916) that she publicly proclaimed her
new allegiance. The piece, whilst sensationalist, is interesting
in that it shows the difficulties the media had in dealing with

Keller. Keller does not refrain from making her views known, and it is in this interview that she publicly calls for revolution and delivers her famous criticism of the Socialist Party as "too slow" and "sinking in the political bog."

Following the entry of the United States into World War I in April 1917, the U.S. Government stepped up suppression of left radicals and their ideas and organizations. Thousands of radicals were arrested and imprisoned and industrial action was violently repressed. Keller responded with *On Behalf of the IWW* (1918), an eloquent and impassioned argument against state suppression of the workers' movement and a justification of the strategy and tactics of the IWW.

Keller found in the IWW an organization that, to a large degree, satisfied her passion and enthusiasm, not to mention her impatience. The radicalism of Keller the "Wobbly" (as the IWWs were known) comes out in her vehement response to a question from the New York *Tribune*: "I don't give a damn about semi-radicals!"

An earlier article, *The Hand of the World* (1912), is included later in Part Two to show the more reflective and poetic side of Keller's politics. It reveals a deep understanding of Marxist labor theory. The use of religious symbolism and metaphor throughout the piece is particularly interesting and a reminder of the spirituality that was also important in her life.

In 1953, during a spate of U.S. Government sponsored anti-communism, communist leader, strike organizer and former Wobbly Elizabeth Gurley Flynn was imprisoned under the Smith Act. In 1955, Flynn's biographer and friend, Muriel Symington, wrote to Keller asking that she write to Flynn in prison on the occasion of her birthday. Keller did so and her rather mild letter provoked considerable publicity in the Cold War hysteria of the time.

Keller was at that time best known as the public face of the American Federation of the Blind (AFB) and the "Gurley Flynn incident" resulted in a number of AFB donors withdrawing their support. The reaction of a Mr. K. Baarslag from Dallas, Texas, was typical. In October 1955 he wrote, in response to a letter from the AFB soliciting donations, "Please remove my name from your mailing. I have long been a great admirer of Miss Keller's work but her letter to communist Elizabeth Gurley Flynn was too much." Following a flood of such letters, AFB Executive Director Robert Irwin wrote to one of his trustees, "Helen Keller's habit of playing around with communists and near communists has long been a source of embarrassment to her conservative friends. Please advise!"

# part three: Women

Keller's approach to the subject of women's liberation clearly has its roots in her socialism. She argues consistently that the issue is not so much patriarchal dominance but a question of class, and that justice and freedom for women, as for the blind and deaf, will only come with the liberation of the working class as a whole. But Keller was certainly a "feminist" in today's under-standing of the term. She agitated for the right to vote, to birth control, equal pay and access to education and she firmly as-serted her own right to be taken seriously as a political thinker and writer.

In the 1910s and 1920s, however, Keller would not have called herself a "feminist," as the term was then understood. In that period there was a sharp delineation between "feminists" who believed that women's equality could be achieved by reforming capitalism, primarily by securing the right to vote, and "revol-utionaries," with whom Keller identified, who saw reforms as necessary but partial steps toward liberation and believed that true liberation could only be won through revolution.

In her *Letter to an English Woman Suffragist* (1911), she writes, "You ask for votes for women. What good can votes do you when ten-elevenths of the land of Great Britain belongs to 200,000, and only one-eleventh to the rest of the 40 million? Have your men with their millions of votes freed themselves from this injustice?" A later article in the *Call, Why Men Need Woman Suffrage* (1913), makes it clear that, although Keller considered votes for women were not the holy grail, she was in fact a strong advocate for women's suffrage. The article, and specifically its title, is also a good example of Keller's subversive sense of humor. With tongue firmly in cheek, she writes, "since masculine chivalry has failed us we must hustle a bit and see what we can do for ourselves..."

In *The New Woman's Party* (1916) she welcomes the formation of a women's political party and writes, "Women have discovered that they cannot rely on men's chivalry to give them justice — just as men before them found out that we cannot be saved by other people — we must save ourselves."

In the 1930s Keller made a living by writing, voluminously, for traditional women's magazines. Most of these later articles avoid any discussion of radical topics although some, like *Great American Women* (1932) reprinted here, show that Keller had not entirely given up agitating for women's rights. The humorous *Put Your Husband in the Kitchen* (1932), is from the same period.

# part four: War

When the United States entered World War I the suppression of leftist organizations increased dramatically. The Espionage Act (1917) and the Sedition Act (1918) made it illegal to publish "disloyal information, express contempt for the government's actions or in any way disrupt or speak publicly against the war." The U.S. Supreme Court would later uphold the legality of serious infringements of freedom of speech on the basis that "when a nation is at war many things that might be said in time of peace are such a hindrance to its efforts that their utterance will not be endured so long as men fight." Dissent was now a treasonable offence.

For Keller, however, the war itself was a product of capitalism's drive for expansion and destruction and she was vocal in her opposition long before the United States committed troops. This opposition was tied closely to her internationalism, particularly evident in her speech *Strike Against War* (1916), an articulate argument that war is waged only for the benefit of "the few who profit from the labor of the masses..." while the poor will be told, "fellow workmen, patriots; your country is in danger!"

A similar theme runs through *The Ford Peace Plan is Doomed to Failure* (1915) in which she writes, "Henry Ford belongs to the same class as the diplomats and politicians that made the war." In *Menace of the Militarist Program* (1915) she observes, "The burden of war always falls heaviest on the toilers. They are taught that their masters can do no wrong, and go out in vast numbers to be killed on the battlefield... If they escape death they come back to face heavy taxation and have their burden of poverty doubled."

Keller's approach remained consistent when the United States began to mobilize troops in Europe. Of particular interest is her letter *To Morris Hillquit (*1917), which makes clear that Keller was no pacifist. Whilst she opposed militarism and what she saw as an unjust war, she did not renounce the use of violence, and even the making of war, in certain circumstances.

> I am not opposed to war for sentimental reasons. The blood of fighting ancestors flows in my veins. I would gladly see our young men go forth to battle if I thought it was a battle for true freedom. I would gladly participate in a war that would really make the world safe for democracy.

Hillquit had been one of the most vocal critics of the IWW from within the Socialist Party and he had initially called for the expulsion of IWW leader Bill Haywood (whom Keller supported) from the Socialist Party's Executive Committee. But Keller puts aside her differences and her qualms about electoralism to declare that, if she had the right to vote (which as a woman she did not) she would vote for Hillquit. She writes: "A vote for you would be a blow at the militarism that is one of the chief bulwarks of capitalism, and the day that militarism is undermined, capitalism will fall."

Both the letter to Hillquit and a later one to *To Eugene V. Debs* (1919) demonstrate Keller's ongoing support for the electoral campaigns of the Socialist Party, despite her previous criticisms. Debs had been arrested for sedition due to his outspoken criticism of the war, and sentenced to 10 years' imprisonment. Keller's letter is in response to the news that Debs' appeal had been overruled.

On the question of the war Keller was in full accord with the Socialist Party. Their internationalist position was by no means shared by the socialist movement as a whole. Many socialists and socialist parties broke with working-class internationalism and supported the war efforts of their capitalist governments. In the process, these parties also broke with revolutionary socialism and began their evolution into reformist, social democratic parties.

After 1922 Keller rarely spoke in public of her socialist convictions, although her private correspondence indicates that she remained firmly on the side of the working class until she died in 1968 at the age of 87. From 1923 until her death she dedicated herself, predominantly, to working with the American Foundation for the Blind as an advocate and fundraiser. The selections in this book are largely from her "rebel years" and do not pretend to reflect the entirety of her life or thinking.

Helen Keller was never imprisoned for her political beliefs — her status as a beloved deafblind icon perhaps gave her some protection in that regard — but her politics were suppressed in other, more insidious ways. In a letter of support to the left independent presidential candidate Robert La Follette, in 1924, she explains her "silence on subjects that are of vital interest to me":

I have hesitated to write to you because I know that the newspapers opposed to the progressive movement will cry out at the "pathetic exploitation of deaf and blind Helen Keller"... So long as I confine my activities to social service and the blind, they compliment me extravagantly, calling me "arch priestess of the sightless," "wonder woman" and "a modern miracle." But when it comes to a discussion of poverty, and I maintain that it is the result of wrong economics — that the industrial system under which we live is at the root of much of the physical deafness and blindness in the world — that is a different matter! It is laudable to give aid to the handicapped. Superficial charities make smooth the way of the prosperous; but to advocate that all human beings should have leisure and comfort, the decencies and refinements of life, is a Utopian dream, and one who seriously contemplates its realization must indeed be deaf, dumb and blind."

*Karen Fletcher and John Davis*
*March 2003*

# chronology

**1880**  Helen Keller born on June 27 in Tuscumbia, Alabama, to former Confederate officer and newspaper publisher Captain Arthur H. Keller and Kate Keller.

**1882**  Loses both sight and hearing as a result of illness.

**1887**  Anne Sullivan hired as Keller's private teacher.

**1900**  Enters Radcliffe College.

**1901**  *I Must Speak* published in the *Ladies' Home Journal*.

**1903**  *Story of My Life* published. First serialized in *The Ladies' Home Journal*, and then as a book.

**1909**  Joins the U.S. Socialist Party in Massachusetts.

**1914**  Demonstrates with the Women's Peace Party for peace in Europe. After the demonstration, makes an impassioned speech against war and for socialism in crowded Carnegie Hall.

**1915**  Denounces Rockefeller as a "monster of capitalism" responsible for the massacre of men, women and children in a bloody confrontation between strikers and the militia at his coal mine in Ludlow, Colorado.

**1916** Announces her support for and membership of the Industrial Workers of the World (IWW).

**1917** Donates money to the National Association for the Advancement of Colored People (NAACP) and writes for the NAACP Journal.

**1918** Helps to found the American Civil Liberties Union (ACLU).

**1919** Plays the part of herself in *Deliverance*, a silent movie about her life and participates in Actors Equity strike associated with the film.

**1924** Supports the presidential campaign of progressive candidate Robert LaFollette.

**1924** Begins work with American Foundation for the Blind (AFB).

**1929** *Midstream: My Later Life* published.

**1936** Anne Sullivan dies October 20.

**1948** Visits the "black, silent hole" that had once been Hiroshima and Nagasaki and speaks out against nuclear war.

**1955** Writes letter of support to Elizabeth Gurley Flynn.

**1961** Suffers stroke and retires from public life.

**1964** Receives the Presidential Medal of Freedom from President Lyndon Johnson.

**1968** Helen Keller dies on June 1 at 87 years of age.

# part one: Disability and Class

## I Must Speak: A Plea to the American Woman

*Ladies' Home Journal* (1901)

A year ago I wrote in the *Ladies' Home Journal* about the prevention of blindness. I wrote guardedly and with hesitation; for the subject was new to me, and I shrank from discussing before the general public a problem which hitherto had been confined to the conferences of specialists. Moreover, the subject was one of which a young woman might be supposed to be ignorant, and upon which, certainly, she would not be expected to speak with authority. It is always painful to set one's self against tradition, especially against the conventions and preju- dices that hedge about womanhood. But continuous study of blindness has forced upon me knowledge of this subject, and, if I am to stand as an advocate of the work for the sightless, I can- not, without accusing myself of cowardice, gloss over or ignore the fundamental evil.

Once I believed that blindness, deafness, tuberculosis and other causes of suffering were necessary, unpreventable. I be- lieved that we must accept blind eyes, deaf ears, diseased lungs as we accept the havoc of tornadoes and deluges, and that we must bear them with as much fortitude as we could gather from religion and philosophy. But gradually my reading extended, and I found that those evils are to be laid not at the door of Providence, but at the door of mankind; that they are, in large measure, due to ignorance, stupidity and sin.

The most common cause of blindness is ophthalmia of the newborn. One pupil in every three at the institution for the blind in New York City was blinded in infancy by this disease. Nearly all of the 16 babies in the Sunshine Home in Brooklyn, one-quarter of the inmates of the New York State Home for the Blind, 600 sightless persons in the state of New York, between 6,000 and 7,000 persons in the United States, were plunged into darkness by ophthalmia of the newborn. The symptoms of the disease appear in the infant's eyes soon after birth. The eyelids swell and become red, and on about the second day they discharge whitish pus. At this stage the eyes can be saved by the simplest prophylactic care. That such care is not always exercised is due to the fact that one-half of the cases of childbirth in America are attended by midwives many of whom are ignorant and incompetent. In this country very little has been done to secure the proper education and examination of midwives; and they and equally ignorant parents resort to poultices, nostrums and domestic remedies.

There is a remedy for ophthalmia neonatorum. This is an instillation of nitrate of silver solution into the eyes of the child. It is efficacious if promptly and skillfully applied. It is not, however, infallible, and in unskillful hands it may do great harm. The mother who sees in the eyes of her baby the symptoms which I have described should lose no time in summoning the assistance of an intelligent physician.

Let no one suppose that this is idle advice. In France and Germany the laws require that the eyes of every child shall be treated with nitrate of silver solution as soon as it is born, and in those countries there has been a considerable decrease in blindness from the scourge of ophthalmia neonatorum. And what do the wise lawmakers of America do? A bill for the prevention of blindness introduced in the Illinois Legislature failed to pass because it was argued that this was only another scheme of doctors to provide fees for themselves! But, at best, the law is concerned only with the remedy. The people themselves, and only they, can wipe out the cause.

What is the cause of ophthalmia neonatorum? It is a specific germ communicated by the mother to the child at birth. Previous to the child's birth she has unconsciously received it through infection from her husband. He has contracted the infection in licentious relations before or since marriage. "The cruelest link in the chain of consequences," says Dr. Prince Morrow, "is the mother's innocent agency. She is made a passive, unconscious medium of instilling into the eyes of her newborn babe a virulent poison which extinguishes its sight."

In mercy let it be remembered, the father does not know that he has so foully destroyed the eyes of his child and handicapped him for life. It is part of the bitter harvest of the wild oats he has sown. Society has smiled upon his "youthful recklessness" because Society does not know that: "They enslave their childen's children who make compromise with sin." Society has yet to learn that the blind beggar at the street corner, the epileptic child, the woman on the operating table, are the wages of "youthful indiscretion." Today science is verifying what the Old Testament taught 3,000 years ago, and the time has come when there is no longer the excuse of ignorance. Knowledge has been given us; it is our part to apply it.

Of the consequences of social sin, blindness is by no means the most terrible. The same infection which blots out the eyes of the baby is responsible for many childless homes; for thousands of cases of lifelong invalidism; for 80 percent of all inflammatory diseases peculiar to women; and for 75 percent of all operations performed on mothers to save their lives.

The day has come when women must face the truth. They cannot escape the consequences of evil unless they have the knowledge that saves. Must we leave young girls to meet the danger in the dark because we dare not turn the light upon our social wickedness? False delicacy and prudery must give place to precise information and common sense. It is high time to abolish falsehood and let the plain truth come in. Out with the cowardice which shuts its eyes to the immorality that causes disease and human misery. I am confident that when the people know the truth the day of deliverance for mother and child will be at hand.

To you, my people, I turn with the faith that you will face the problem and work out the salvation of your children. We must look to it that every child is protected before his birth. Every child has a right to be well born. Every child has a right to be told by his parents and teachers about his birth and his body; for in such knowledge lie true innocence and safety. Civilization is menaced by an insidious enemy. It must learn that only one cure is sure and cheap: right living, which God gives free to all. And right living depends on right knowledge.

We must set to work in the right direction the three great agencies which inform and educate us: the church, the school and the press. If they remain silent, obdurate, they will bear the odium which recoils upon evildoers. They may not listen at first to our plea for light and knowledge. They may combine to baffle us; but there will rise, again and again, to confront them, the beseeching forms of little children: deaf, blind, crooked of limb and vacant of mind.

My countrywomen, this is not faultfinding. I am not a pessimist, but an optimist, by temperament and conviction. I am making a plea for American women and their children. I plead that the blind may see, the deaf may hear, and the idiot may have a mind. In a word, I plead that the American woman may be the mother of a great race.

Throw aside, I beseech you, false modesty — the shame that shelters evil — and hasten the day when there shall be no preventable disease among mankind.

# Social Causes of Blindness
New York *Call* (1911)

I rejoice that the greatest of all work for the blind, the saving of eyesight, has been laid so clearly before the public. The reports of progress in the conservation of eyes, of health, of life, of all things precious to men are as a trumpet blast summoning us to still greater effort. The devotion of physicians and laymen, and the terrible needs of our fellow men ought to hearten us in the fight against conquerable misery.

Our worst foes are ignorance, poverty and the unconscious cruelty of our commercial society. These are the causes of much blindness, these are the enemies which destroy the sight of little children and workmen, and undermine the health of mankind. So long as these enemies remain unvanquished, so long will there be blind and crippled men and women.

To study the diseases and accidents by which sight is lost, and to learn how the surgeon can prevent or alleviate them, is not enough. We must strive to put an end to the conditions which cause the disease and accidents.

This case of blindness, the physician says, resulted from ophthalmia. It was really caused by a dark, overcrowded room, by the indecent herding together of human beings in insanitary tenements. We are told that another case was produced by the bursting of a wheel. The real cause was an employer's failure to safeguard his machines. Investigation shows that there are many clever safeguards for machinery which ought to be used in factories, but which are not adopted because their adoption would diminish the employer's profits.

Labor reports indicate that we Americans have been slow, dishonorably slow, in taking measures for the protection of our workmen.

Does it occur to you that the white lace which we wear is darkened by the failing eyes of the lacemaker? The trouble is that we do not understand the essential relation between poverty and disease. I do not believe that there is anyone in this city of kind hearts who would willingly receive dividends if he knew that they were paid in part with blinded eyes and broken backs. If you doubt that there is such a connection between our prosperity and the sorrows of the poor, consult those bare but illuminated reports of industrial commissions and labor bureaus. They are less eloquent than oratory. In them you will find the fundamental causes of much blindness and crookedness, of shrunken limbs and degraded minds. These causes must be searched out, and every condition in which blindness breeds must be exposed and abolished. Let our battle cry be: "No preventable disease, no unnecessary poverty, no blinding ignorance among mankind."

# The Unemployed

*Zeigler Magazine for the Blind* (1911)

Some time ago I received a pathetic letter from a workman in a woolen mill. I quote a part of it:

> I was employed in the worsted trade in England before coming
> to this country. I had worked for 10 years and learned a good
> deal about wool, tops and noils. I came to this country in the
> hope of climbing the industrial ladder. I could hear pretty well,
> or I should not have passed the immigration officers. I got work

quickly at the very bottom of the ladder. I kept my eyes open and learned everything that came my way, and in time I was transferred to the combing room to learn to be a section hand. By this time my hearing had become slightly worse. All the help in this department were either Italians or Poles, so that between their broken English and my defective hearing I was much handicapped. I have been on short time for over a year, and since the new year I have earned $6.71 per week. There are six of us to feed, clothe and shelter, and coal to buy. How to find a bare existence is the problem that confronts me today. I would take anything where I could earn steady pay. I have the idea that I shall yet rise out of the mire. But in the meantime I must live and support my family, and this I cannot do under present circumstances.

This workman is deaf, but his position is similar to that of many of the sightless. We have been accustomed to regard the unemployed deaf and blind as victims of their infirmities. This is to say, we have supposed that if their sight and hearing were miraculously restored, they would find work. The problem of the underpaid and underemployed workman is too large to discuss here. But I wish to suggest to the readers of this article that the unemployment of the blind is only part of a greater problem.

There are, it is estimated, a million laborers out of work in the United States. Their inaction is not due to physical defects or lack of ability or of intelligence, or to ill health or vice. It is due to the fact that our present system of production necessitates a large margin of idle men. The business world in which we live cannot give every man opportunity to fulfil his capabilities or even assure him continuous occupation as an unskilled laborer. The means of employment — the land and the factories, that is, the tools of labor — are in the hands of a minority of the people, and are used rather with a view to increasing the owner's profits than with a view to keeping all men busy and productive. Hence there are more men than jobs. This is the first and the chief evil of the so-called capitalistic system of production. The workman has nothing to sell but his labor. He is in strife, in rivalry with his fellows for a chance to sell his power. Naturally the weaker workman is thrust aside. That does not mean that he is utterly incapacitated for industrial activity, but only that he is less capable than his successful competitor.

In the majority of cases there is no relation between unemployment and ability. A factory shuts down and all the operatives, the more competent as well as the less competent, are thrown out of work. In February the cotton mill owners of Massachusetts agreed to run the mills on a schedule of four days a week. The employees were not to blame for the reduction of work, nor were the employers to blame. The considerations of the market compelled it.

Thus, it has come to pass that in this land of plenty there is an increasing number of "superfluous men." The doors of industry are closed to them the whole year or part of the year. No less than six million American men, women and the children are in a permanent state of want because of total or partial idleness. In a small corner of this vast social distress we find our unemployed blind. Their lack of sight is not the primary cause of their idleness; it is a contributing cause; it relegates them to the enormous army of the unwilling idle.

We can subsidize the work of the sightless; we can build special institutions and factories for them, and solicit the help of wealthy patrons. But the blind man cannot become an independent, self-supporting member of society, he can never do all that he is capable of, until all his seeing brothers have opportunities to work to the full extent of their ability. We know now that the welfare of the whole people is essential to the welfare of each. We know that the blind are not debarred from usefulness solely by their infirmity. Their idleness is fundamentally caused by conditions which press heavily upon all working people, and deprive hundreds of thousands of good men of a livelihood.

I recommend that all who are interested in the economic problem of the sightless study the economic problem of the seeing. Let us begin with such books as Mr. Robert Hunter's *Poverty,* and Edmond Kelly's *Twentieth Century Socialism.* Let us read these books, not for "theory," as it is sometimes scornfully called, but for facts about the labor conditions in America. Mr. Kelly was a teacher of political economy, a lecturer on municipal government at Columbia University. Mr. Hunter has spent many years studying the American workman in his home and in the shop. The facts which they spread before us show that it is not physical blindness, but social blindness which cheats our hands of the right to toil.

# To the Strikers at Little Falls, New York
*Solidarity* (1912)

I am sending the check which Mr. Davis paid me for the Christmas sentiments I sent him. Will you give it to the brave girls who are striving so courageously to bring about the emancipation of the workers at Little Falls?

They have my warmest sympathy. Their cause is my cause. If they are denied a living wage, I also am denied. While they are industrial slaves, I cannot be free. My hunger is not satisfied while they are unfed. I cannot enjoy the good things of life which come to me, if they are hindered and neglected. I want all the workers of the world to have sufficient money to provide the elements of a normal standard of living: a decent home, healthful surroundings, opportunity for education and recreation. I want them all to have the same blessings that I have. I, deaf and blind, have been helped to overcome many obstacles. I want them to be helped as generously in a struggle which resembles my own in many ways.

Surely the things that the workers demand are not unreasonable. It cannot be unreasonable to ask of society a fair chance for all. It cannot be unreasonable to demand the protection of women and little children and an honest wage for all who give their time and energy to industrial occupations. When indeed shall we learn that we are all related one to the other, that we are all members of one body? Until the spirit of love for our fellow men, regardless of race, color or creed, shall fill the world, making real in our lives and our deeds the actuality of human brotherhood, until the great mass of the people shall be filled with the sense of responsibility for each other's welfare, social justice can never be attained.

# Comments to the House Committee on Labor

(1944)

Members of the House Committee On Labor,

Nothing could please me more than to speak here this morning as it gives me an opportunity to direct your attention once more to the consideration of a handicap allowance for the blind. Fully I endorse it as expressing the best thought of our day concerning the needs and difficulties of those who cannot see. You will, I am sure, be favorably disposed towards this constructive effort.

Dr. Robert B. Irwin, Executive Director of the American Foundation for the Blind (AFB), has clearly shown in his testimony before your committee at its hearings in Washington, [that] the Social Security Act has not provided sufficiently for the particular needs of the poorer blind, or taken into account their severe curtailments in breadwinning opportunities and personal liberty. As a result they must incur unaided peculiar expenses which lack of sight entails. For instance they must pay a guide or a reader at the sacrifice of other precious necessaries. Most of them cannot afford Braille writers or typewriters. Can you imagine yourself in the dark, unable to send a written message to a son or a brother overseas or to a friend at home?

There are two groups of the blind who should have an adequate handicap allowance and for whom I especially plead. One is the colored blind. In my travels up and down the continent I have visited their shabby school buildings and witnessed their pathetic struggle against want. I have been shocked by the meagerness of their education, lack of proper medical care and the discrimination which limits their employment chances. I feel it a disgrace that in this great wealthy land such injustice should exist to men and women of a different race — and blind at that! It is imperative that colored people without sight be granted financial aid worthy of their human dignity and courage in the face of fearful obstacles.

The other group, the deafblind, is small but heartbreaking to contemplate. They are tragically isolated, and it is difficult to arouse enough interest to soften their fate. They are scattered, it is hard to find out how many of them there are. Even if the deafblind are taught, how seldom anyone offers to entertain them or gladden them with pleasant companionship! In every state there is an agency trained and willing to help the blind in their economic problems and diversions, but not one has been organized to rehabilitate the loneliest people on earth, those without sight or hearing. They have no funds to buy little advantages or enjoyments that would bring sunshine in their double dungeon — darkness and silence. If we are not to be haunted by remorse and shame at all our blessings while they have nothing, a definite effort must be started to raise them from the ultimate disaster to life's goodness and friendship's consolation.

What I ask of you is to use your influence to revise the Social

Security Act so that it may minister generously to the hardest pressed and the least cared for among my blind fellows. If you do, the sight and liberty you enjoy will be all the sweeter to you.

[Speech delivered before the Subcommittee on Labor to Investigate Aid to Physically Handicapped at New York.]

# part two: Socialism

## How I Became a Socialist

New York *Call* (1912)

For several months my name and socialism have appeared often together in the newspapers. A friend tells me that I have shared the front pages with baseball, Mr. Roosevelt and the New York police scandal. The association does not make me altogether happy but, on the whole, I am glad that many people are interested in me and in the educational achievements of my teacher, Mrs. Macy. Even notoriety may be turned to beneficent uses, and I rejoice if the disposition of the newspapers to record my activities results in bringing more often into their columns the word socialism. In the future I hope to write about socialism, and to justify in some measure the great amount of publicity which has been accorded to me and my opinions. So far I have written little and said little about the subject. I have written a few letters, notably one to Comrade Fred Warren which was printed in the *Appeal to Reason*. I have talked to some reporters, one of whom, Mr. Ireland of the *New York World*, made a very flattering report and gave fully and fairly what I said. I have never been in Schenectady. I have never met Mayor Lunn. I have never had a letter from him, but he has sent kind messages to me through Mr. Macy. Owing to Mrs. Macy's illness, whatever plans I had to join the workers in Schenectady have been abandoned.

On such negative and relatively insignificant matters have been written many editorials in the capitalist press and in the socialist press. The clippings fill a drawer. I have not read a quarter of them, and I doubt if I shall ever read them all. If on such a small quantity of fact so much comment has followed, what will the newspapers do if I ever set to work in earnest to write and talk on behalf of socialism? For the present I should like to make a statement of my position and correct some false reports and answer some criticisms which seem to me unjust.

First, how did I become a socialist? By reading. The first book I read was Wells' *New Worlds for Old.* I read it on Mrs. Macy's recommendation. She was attracted by its imaginative quality, and hoped that its electric style might stimulate and interest me. When she gave me the book, she was not a socialist and she is not a socialist now. Perhaps she will be one before Mr. Macy and I are done arguing with her.

Mr. Wells led to others. I asked for more books on the subject, and Mr. Macy selected some from his library of socialist literature. He did not urge them on me. He merely complied with my request for more. I do not find him inclined to instruct me about socialism; indeed, I have often complained to him that he did not talk to me about it as much as I should like. My reading has been limited and slow. I take German bimonthly socialist periodicals printed in Braille for the blind. (Our German comrades are ahead of us in many respects.) I have also in German Braille Kautsky's discussion of the Erfurt Program. The other socialist literature that I have read has been spelled into my hand by a friend who comes three times a week to read to me whatever I choose to have read. The periodical which I have most often requested her lively fingers to communicate to my eager ones is the *National Socialist.* She gives the titles of the articles and I tell her when to read on and when to omit. I have also had her read to me from the *International Socialist Review* articles the titles of which sounded promising. Manual spelling takes time. It is no easy and rapid thing to absorb through one's fingers a book of 50,000 words on economics. But it is a pleasure, and one which I shall enjoy repeatedly until I have made myself acquainted with all the classic socialist authors.

In the light of the foregoing I wish to comment on a piece about me which was printed in the *Common Cause* and reprinted in the *Live Issue,* two antisocialist publications. Here is a quotation from that piece:

> For 25 years Miss Keller's teacher and constant companion has been Mrs. John Macy, formerly of Wrentham, Massachusetts. Both Mr. and Mrs. Macy are enthusiastic Marxist propagandists, and it is scarcely surprising that Miss Keller, depending upon this lifelong friend for her most intimate knowledge of life, should have imbibed such opinions.

Mr. Macy may be an enthusiastic Marxist propagandist, though I am sorry to say he has not shown much enthusiasm in propagating his Marxism through my fingers. Mrs. Macy is not a Marxist, nor a socialist. Therefore what the *Common Cause* says about her is not true. The editor must have invented that, made it out of whole cloth, and if that is the way his mind works, it is no wonder that he is opposed to socialism. He has not sufficient sense of fact to be a socialist or anything else intellectually worthwhile. Consider another quotation from the same article. The headline reads:

SCHENECTADY REDS ARE ADVERTIZING, USING HELEN KELLER,
THE BLIND GIRL, TO RECEIVE PUBLICITY

Then the article begins:

> It would be difficult to imagine anything more pathetic than the

present exploitation of poor Helen Keller by the socialists of Schenectady. For weeks the party's press agencies have heralded the fact that she is a socialist, and is about to become a member of Schenectady's new Board of Public Welfare.

There's a chance for satirical comment on the phrase, "the exploitation of poor Helen Keller." But I will refrain, simply saying that I do not like the hypocritical sympathy of such a paper as the *Common Cause,* but I am glad if it knows what the word "exploitation" means.

Let us come to the facts. When Mayor Lunn heard that I might go to Schenectady he proposed to the Board of Public Welfare that a place be kept on it for me. Nothing was printed about this in *The Citizen,* Mayor Lunn's paper. Indeed, it was the intention of the board to say nothing about the matter until after I had moved to Schenectady. But the reporters of the capitalist press got wind of the plan, and one day, during Mayor Lunn's absence from Schenectady, the *Knickerbocker Press* of Albany made the announcement.

It was telegraphed all over the country, and then began the real newspaper exploitation. By the socialist press? No, by the capitalist press. The socialist papers printed the news, and some of them wrote editorials of welcome. But *The Citizen,* Mayor Lunn's paper, preserved silence and did not mention my name during all the weeks when the reporters were telephoning and telegraphing and asking for interviews. It was the capitalist press that did the exploiting. Why? Because ordinary newspapers care anything about socialism? No, of course not; they hate it. But because, alas, I am a subject for newspaper gossip. We got so tired of denying that I was in Schenectady that I began to dislike the reporter who first published the "news."

The socialist papers, it is true, did make a good deal of me after the capitalist papers had "heralded the fact that I am a socialist." But all the reporters who came to see me were from ordinary commercial newspapers. No socialist paper, neither the *Call* nor the *National Socialist* ever asked me for an article. The editor of *The Citizen* hinted to Mr. Macy that he would like one, but he was too fine and considerate to ask for it point-blank.

The *New York Times* did ask me for one. The editor of the *Times* wrote assuring me that his paper was a valuable medium for reaching the public and he wanted an article from me. He also telegraphed asking me to send him an account of my plans and to outline my ideas of my duties as a member of the Board of Public Welfare of Schenectady. I am glad I did not comply with this request, for some days later the *Times* made me a social outcast beyond the range of its righteous sympathies. On September 21 there appeared in the *Times* an editorial called "The Contemptible Red Flag." I quote two passages from it:

> The flag is free. But it is nonetheless detestable. It is the symbol of lawlessness and anarchy the world over, and as such is held in contempt by all right-minded persons.
>
> The bearer of a red flag may not be molested by the police until he commits some act which the red flag justifies. He deserves, however, always to be regarded with suspicion. By carrying the symbol of lawlessness he forfeits all right to respect and sympathy.

I am no worshiper of cloth of any color, but I love the red flag and what is symbolizes to me and other socialists. I have a red flag hanging in my study, and if I could I should gladly march with it past the office of the *Times* and let all the reporters and photographers make the most of the spectacle. According to the inclusive condemnation of the *Times* I have forfeited all right to respect and sympathy, and I am to be regarded with suspicion. Yet the editor of the *Times* wants me to write him an article. How can he trust me to write for him if I am a suspicious character? I hope you will enjoy as much as I do the bad ethics, bad logic, bad manners that a capitalist editor falls into when he tries to condemn the movement which is aimed at his plutocratic interests. We are not entitled to sympathy, yet some of us can write articles that will help his paper to make money. Probably our opinions have the same sort of value to him that he would find in the confession of a famous murderer. We are not nice, but we are interesting.

I like newspapermen. I have known many, and two or three editors have been among my most intimate friends. Moreover, the newspapers have been of great assistance in the work which we have been trying to do for the blind. It costs them nothing to give their aid to work for the blind and to other superficial charities. But socialism — ah, that is a different matter! That goes to the root of all poverty and all charity. The money power behind the newspapers is against socialism, and the editors, obedient to the hand that feeds them, will go to any length to put down socialism and undermine the influence of socialists.

When my letter to Comrade Fred Warren was published in the *Appeal to Reason,* a friend of mine who writes a special department for the Boston *Transcript* made an article about it and the editor-in-chief cut it out.

The Brooklyn *Eagle* says, apropos of me, and socialism, that Helen Keller's "mistakes spring out of the manifest limitations of her development." Some years ago I met a gentleman who was introduced to me as Mr. McKelway, editor of the Brooklyn *Eagle.* It was after a meeting that we had in New York on behalf of the blind. At that time the compliments he paid me were so generous that I blush to remember them. But now that I have come out for socialism he reminds me and the public that I am blind and deaf and especially liable to error. I must have shrunk in intelligence during the years since I met him. Surely it his turn to blush. It may be that deafness and blindness incline one toward socialism. Marx was probably stone deaf and William Morris was blind. Morris painted his pictures by the sense of touch and designed wallpaper by the sense of smell.

Oh, ridiculous Brooklyn *Eagle!* What an ungallant bird it is! Socially blind and deaf, it defends an intolerable system, a system that is the cause of much of the physical blindness and deafness which we are trying to prevent. The *Eagle* is willing to help us prevent misery provided, always provided, that we do not attack the industrial tyranny which supports it and stops its ears and clouds its vision. The *Eagle* and I are at war. I hate the system which it represents, apologizes for and upholds. When it fights back, let it fight fair. Let it attack my ideas and oppose the aims and arguments of socialism. It is not fair fighting or good argument to remind me and others that I cannot see or hear. I can read. I can read all the socialist books I have time for in English, German and French. If the editor of the Brooklyn *Eagle* should read some of them, he might be a wiser man and make a better newspaper. If I ever contribute to the socialist movement the book that I sometimes dream of, I know what I shall name it: *Industrial Blindness and Social Deafness.*

# Why I Became an IWW

Interview with Helen Keller by Barbara Bindley
New York *Tribune*, (1916)

I asked that Miss Keller relate the steps by which she turned into the uncompromising radical who now faces the world as Helen Keller, not the sweet sentimentalist of women's magazine days.

"I was religious to start with," she began in enthusiastic acquiescence to my request. "I had thought blindness a misfortune."

"Then I was appointed on a commission to investigate the conditions among the blind. For the first time I, who had thought blindness a misfortune beyond human control, found that too much of it was traceable to wrong industrial conditions, often caused by the selfishness and greed of employers. And the social evil contributed its share. I found that poverty drove women to the life of shame that ended in blindness.

"Then I read H.G. Wells' *Old Worlds for New,* summaries of Karl Marx's philosophy and his manifestoes. It seemed as if I had been asleep and waked to a new world — a world so different from the beautiful world I had lived in.

"For a time I was depressed" — her voice saddened in reminiscence — "but little by little my confidence came back and I realized that the wonder is not that conditions are so bad, but that humanity has advanced so far in spite of them. And now I am in the fight to change things. I may be a dreamer, but dreamers are necessary to make facts!" Her voice almost shrilled in its triumph, and her hand found and clutched my knee in vibrant emphasis.

"And you feel happier than in the beautiful make-believe world you had dreamed?" I questioned.

"Yes," she answered with firm finality in the voice which stumbles a little. "Reality even when it is sad is better than illusions." (This from a woman whom it would seem all earthly things are but that.) "Illusions are at the mercy of any winds that blow. Real happiness must come from within, from a fixed purpose and faith in one's fellow men, and of that I have more than I ever had."

"And all this had to come after you left college? Did you get none of this knowledge of life at college?"

"No!" — an emphatic, triumphant, almost terrifying denial — college isn't the place to go for any ideas. "I thought I was going to college to be educated," she resumed as she composed herself, and laughing more lightly, "I am an example of the education dealt out to present generations. It's a deadlock. Schools seem to love the dead past and live in it."

"But you know, don't you," I pleaded through Mrs. Macy and for her, "that the intentions of your teachers were of the best."

"But they amounted to nothing," she countered. "They did not teach me about things as they are today, or about the vital problems of the people. They taught me Greek drama and Roman history, they celebrated achievements of war rather than those of the heroes of peace. For instance, there were a dozen chapters on war where there were a few paragraphs about the inventors, and it is this overemphasis of the cruelties of life that breeds the wrong ideal. Education taught me that it was a finer thing to be a Napoleon than to create a new potato.

"It is my nature to fight as soon as I see wrongs to be made right. So after I read Wells and Marx and learned what I did, I joined a Socialist [Party] branch. I made up my mind to do something. And the best thing seemed to join a fighting party and help their propaganda. That was four years ago. I have been an industrialist since."

"An industrialist?" I asked, surprised out of composure. "You don't mean an IWW — a syndicalist?"

"I became an IWW because I found out that the Socialist Party was too slow. It is sinking in the political bog. It is almost, if not quite, impossible for the party to keep its revolutionary character so long as it occupies a place under the government and seeks office under it. The government does not stand for interests the Socialist Party is supposed to represent."

Socialism, however, is a step in the right direction, she conceded to her dissenting hearers.

"The true task is to unite and organize all workers on an economic basis, and it is the workers themselves who must secure freedom for themselves, who must grow strong," Miss Keller continued. "Nothing can be gained by political action. That is why I became an IWW."

"What particular incident led you to become an IWW?" I interrupted.

"The Lawrence strike. Why? Because I discovered that the true idea of the IWW is not only to better conditions, to get them for all people, but to get them at once."

"What are you committed to — education or revolution?"

"Revolution." She answered decisively. "We can't have education without revolution. We have tried education for 1,900 years and it has failed. Let us try revolution and see what it will do now.

"I am not for peace at all hazards. I regret this war, but I have never regretted the blood of the thousands spilled during the French Revolution. And the workers are learning how to stand alone. They are learning a lesson they will apply to their own good out in the trenches. Generals testify to the splendid initiative the workers in the trenches take. If they can do that for their masters you can be sure they will do that for themselves when they have taken matters into their own hands.

"And don't forget workers are getting their discipline in the trenches," Miss Keller continued. "They are acquiring the will to combat. My cause will emerge from the trenches stronger than it ever was. Under the obvious battle waging there, there is an invisible battle for the freedom of man."

And this finally from the patience-exhausted, gentle little woman: "I don't give a damn about semi-radicals!"

Gradually, through the talk, Helen Keller's whole being had taken on a glow, and it was in keeping with the exalted look on her face and the glory in her sightless blue eyes that she told me:

"I feel like Joan of Arc at times. My whole [being] becomes uplifted. I, too, hear the voices that say 'Come,' and I will follow, no matter what the cost, no matter what the trials I am placed under. Jail, poverty, calumny — they matter not. Truly He has said, 'Woe unto you that permits the least of mine to suffer.' "

# What is the IWW?

New York *Call* (1918)

I am going to talk about the Industrial Workers of the World (IWW) because they are so much in the public eye just now. They are probably the most hated and most loved organization in existence. Certainly they are the least understood and the most persistently misrepresented.

The IWW is a labor union based on the class struggle. It admits only wage earners, and acts on the principle of industrial unionism. Its battleground is the field of industry. The visible expression of the battle is the strike, the lockout, the clash between employer and employed. It is a movement of revolt against the ignorance, the poverty, the cruelty that too many of us accept in blind content.

It was founded in 1905 by men of bitter experience in the labor struggle, and in 1909 it began to attract nationwide attention. The McKees Rocks strike first brought it to notice. The textile strike of Lawrence, Massachusetts, the silk workers' strike of Paterson, New Jersey, and the miners' strike of Calumet, Michigan, made it notorious. Since 1909 it has been a militant force in America that employers have had to reckon with.

It differs from the trade unions in that it emphasizes the idea of one big union of all industries in the economic field. It points out that the trade unions as presently organized are an obstacle to unity among the masses, and that this lack of solidarity plays into the hands of their economic masters.

The IWWs affirm as a fundamental principle that the creators of wealth are entitled to all they create. Thus they find themselves pitted against the whole profit making system. They declare that there can be no compromise so long as the majority of the working class lives in want while the master class lives in luxury. They insist that there can be no peace until the workers organize as a class, take possession of the resources of the earth and the machinery of production and distribution and abolish the wage system. In other words, the workers in their collectivity must own and operate all the essential industrial institutions and secure to each laborer the full value of his product.

It is for these principles, this declaration of class solidarity, that the IWWs are being persecuted, beaten, imprisoned, murdered. If the capitalist class had the sense it is reputed to have, it would know that violence is the worst weapon that can be used against men who have nothing to lose and the world to gain.

Let me tell you something about the IWWs as I see them. They are the unskilled, the ill-paid, the unnaturalized [immigrants], the submerged part of the working class. They are mostly composed of textile mill workers, lumbermen, harvesters, miners, transport workers. We are told that they are "foreigners," "the scum of the earth," "dangerous."

Many of them are foreigners simply because the greater part of the unskilled labor in this country is foreign. "Scum of the earth?" Perhaps. I know they have never had a fair chance. They have been starved in body and mind, denied, exploited, driven like slaves from job to job. "Dangerous?" Maybe. They have endured countless wrongs and injuries until they are driven to rebellion. They know that the laws are for the strong, that they protect the class that owns everything. They know that in a contest with the workers, employers do not respect the laws, but quite shamelessly break them.

Witness the lynching of Frank Little in Butte; the flogging of 17 men in Tulsa; the forcible deportation of 1,200 miners from Bisbee; the burning to death of women and little children in the tents of Ludlow, Colorado; and the massacre of workers in Trinidad. So the IWWs respect the law only as a soldier respects an enemy! Can you find it in your hearts to blame them? I love them for their needs, their miseries, their endurance and their daring spirit. It is because of this spirit that the master class fears and hates them. It is because of this spirit that the poor and oppressed love them with a great love.

The oft-repeated charge that the IWW is organized to hinder industry is false. It is organized in order to keep industries going. By organizing industrially they are forming the structure of the new society in the shell of the old.

Industry rests on the iron law of economic determination. All history reveals that economic interests are the strongest ties that bind men together. That is not because men's hearts are evil and selfish. It is only a result of the inexorable law of life. The desire to live is the basic principle that compels men and women to seek a more suitable environment, so that they may live better and more happily.

Now, don't you see, it is impossible to maintain an economic order that keeps wages practically at a standstill, while the cost of living mounts higher and even higher? Remember, the day will come when the tremendous activities of the war will subside. Capitalism will inevitably find itself face to face with a starving multitude of unemployed workers demanding food or destruction of the social order that has starved them and robbed them of their jobs.

In such a crisis the capitalist class cannot save itself or its institutions. Its police and armies will be powerless to put down the last revolt. For man at last will take his own, not considering the cost. When that day dawns, if the workers are not thoroughly organized, they may easily become a blind force of destruction, unable to check their own momentum, their cry for justice drowned in a howl of rage. Whatever is good and beneficent in our civilization can be saved only by the workers. And the IWW is formed with the object of carrying on the business of the world when capitalism is overthrown. Whether the IWW increases in power or is crushed out of existence, the spirit that animates it is the spirit that must animate the labor movement if it is to have a revolutionary function.

# On Behalf of the IWW
*The Liberator* (1918)

Down through the long weary years the will of the ruling class has been to suppress either the man or his message when they antagonized its interests. From the execution of the propagandist and the burning of books, down through the various degrees of censorship and expurgation to the highly civilized legal indictment and winking at mob crime by constituted authorities, the cry has ever been "crucify him!" The ideas and activities of minorities are misunderstood and misrepresented. It is easier to condemn than to investigate. It takes courage to steer one's course through a storm of abuse and ignominy. But I believe that discussion of even the most bitterly controverted matters is demanded by our love of justice, by our sense of fairness and an honest desire to understand the problems that are rending society. Let us review the facts relating to the situation of the Industrial Workers of the World (IWWs) since the United States entered the war with the declared purpose to conserve the liberties of the free peoples of the world.

During the last few months, in Washington State, at Pasco and throughout the Yakima Valley, many Industrial Workers of the World (IWW) members have been arrested without warrants, thrown into "bullpens" without access to attorney, denied bail and trial by jury, and some of them shot. Did any of the leading newspapers denounce these acts as unlawful, cruel, undemocratic? No. On the contrary, most of them indirectly praised the perpetrators of these crimes for their patriotic service!

On August 1, 1917, in Butte, Montana, a cripple, Frank Little, a member of the executive board of the IWW, was forced out of bed at three in the morning by masked citizens, dragged behind an automobile and hanged on a railroad trestle. Were the offenders punished? No. A high government official has publicly condoned this murder, thereby upholding lynch law and mob rule.

On July 12, 1,200 miners were deported from Bisbee, Arizona, without legal process. Among them were many who were not IWWs or even in sympathy with them. They were all packed into freight cars like cattle and flung upon the desert of New Mexico, where they would have died of thirst and hunger if an outraged society had not protested. President Wilson telegraphed the governor of Arizona that it was a bad thing to do, and a commission was sent to investigate. But nothing has been done. No measures have been taken to return the miners to their homes and families.

Last September 5, an army of officials raided every hall and office of the IWW from Maine to California. They rounded up 166 IWW officers, members and sympathizers, and now they are in jail in Chicago, awaiting trial on the general charge of conspiracy.

In a short time these men will be tried in a Chicago court. The newspapers will be full of stupid, if not malicious, comments on their trial. Let us keep an open mind. Let us try to preserve the integrity of our judgment against the misrepresentation, ignorance and cowardice of the day. Let us refuse to yield to conventional lies and censure. Let us keep our hearts tender toward those who are struggling mightily against the greatest evils of the age. Who is truly indicted, they or the social system that has produced them? A society that permits the conditions out of which the IWWs have sprung, stands self-condemned.

The IWW is pitted against the whole profit making system. It insists that there can be no compromise so long as the majority of the working class lives in want, while the master class lives in luxury. According to its statement: "there can be no peace until the workers organize as a class, take possession of the resources of the earth and the machinery of production and distribution, and abolish the wage system." In other words, the workers in their collectivity must own and operate all the essential industrial institutions and secure to each laborer the full value of his produce.

I think it is for this declaration of democratic purpose, and not for any wish to betray their country, that the IWW members are being persecuted, beaten, imprisoned and murdered.

Surely the demands of the IWW are just. It is right that the creators of wealth should own what they create. When shall we learn that we are related one to the other, that we are members of one body, that injury to one is injury to all? Until the spirit of love for our fellow workers, regardless of race, color, creed or sex, shall fill the world, until the great mass of the people shall be filled with a sense of responsibility for each other's welfare, social justice cannot be attained, and there can never be lasting peace upon earth.

I know those men are hungry for more life, more opportunity. They are tired of the hollow mockery of mere existence in a world of plenty. I am glad of every effort that the workingmen make to organize. I realize that all things will never be better until they are organized, until they stand together like one man. That is my hope of world democracy. Despite their errors, their blunders and the ignominy heaped upon them, I sympathize with the IWWs. Their cause is my cause. While they are threatened and imprisoned, I am manacled. If they are denied a living wage, I too am defrauded. While they are industrial slaves, I cannot be free. My hunger is not satisfied while they are unfed. I cannot enjoy the good things of life that come to me while they are hindered and neglected.

The mighty mass movement of which they are a part is discernible all over the world. Under the fire of the great guns, the workers of all lands, becoming conscious of their class, are preparing to take possession of their own.

That long struggle in which they have successively won freedom of body from slavery and serfdom, freedom of mind from ecclesiastical despotism, and more recently a voice in government, has arrived at a new stage. The workers are still far from being in possession of themselves or their labor. They do not own and control the tools and materials which they must use in order to live, nor do they receive anything like the full value of what they produce. Workingmen everywhere are becoming aware that they are being exploited for the benefit of others, and that they cannot be truly free unless they own themselves and their labor. The achievement of such economic freedom stands in prospect — and at no distant date — as the revolutionary climax of the age.

# The Hand of the World

*American* magazine (1912)

The symbol, sign and instrument
Of each soul's purpose, passion, strife,
Of fires in which are poured and spent
Their all of love, their all of life.
O feeble, mighty human hand!
O fragile, dauntless human heart!
The universe holds nothing planned
With such sublime, transcendent art!
        —Helen Fiske Jackson

As I write this, I am sitting in a pleasant house, in a sunny, wide-windowed study filled with plants and flowers. Here I sit warmly clad, secure against want, sure that what my welfare requires the world will give. Through these generous surroundings I feel the touch of a hand, invisible but potent, all sustaining; the hand that wove my garments, the hand that stretched the roof over my head, the hand that printed the pages I read.

What is that hand which shelters me? In vain the winds buffet my house and hurl the biting cold against the windows: that hand still keeps me warm. What is it, that I may lean upon it at every step I take in the dark, and it fails me not? I give wondering praise to the beneficent hand that ministers to my joy and comfort, that toils for the daily bread of all. I would gratefully acknowledge my debt to its capability and kindness. I pray that some hearts may heed my words about the hand of the world, that they may believe in the coming of that commonwealth in which the gyves [chains] shall be struck from the wrist of labor, and the pulse of production shall be strong with joy.

All our earthly well being hangs upon the living hand of the world. Society is founded upon it. Its lifebeats throb in our institutions. Every industry, every process, is wrought by a hand, or by a superhand; a machine whose mighty arm and cunning fingers the human hand invents and wields. The hand embodies its skill, projects and multiplies itself, in wondrous tools, and with them it spins and weaves, plows and reaps, converts clay into walls, and roofs our habitations with trees of the forest. It compels titans of steel to heave incredible burdens, and commands the service of nimble lackeys which neither groan nor become exhausted. Communication between mind and mind, between writer and reader is made possible by marvelous extensions of the might of the hand, by elaborate reduplications of the many-motioned fingers. I have touched one of those great printing presses in which a river of paper flows over the type, is cut, folded, and piled with swift precision. Between my thoughts and the words which you read on this page a thousand hands have intervened; a hundred shafts of steel have rocked to and fro, to and fro in industrious rhythm.

The hand of the world! Think how it sends forth the waters where it will to form canals between the seas, and binds the same seas with thoughts incorporated in arms of stone! What is the telegraph cable but the quick hand of the world extended between the nations, now menacing, now clasped in brotherhood? What are our ships and railways but the feet of man made swift and strong by his hands? The hand captures the winds, the sun and the lightnings, and dispatches them upon errands of commerce. Before its irresistible blows, mountains are beaten small as dust. Huge derricks — prehensile power magnified in digits of steel — rear factories and palaces, lay stone upon stone in our stately monuments, and raise cathedral spires.

On the hand of the world are visible the records of biology, of history, of all human existence since the day of the "first thumb that caught the trick of thought." Every hand wears a birth seal. By the lines of the thumb each of us can be identified from infancy to age. So by the marks on the bands of the world its unmistakable personality is revealed. Through suffering and prosperity, through periods of retrograde and progress, the hand keeps its identity. Even now, when the ceaseless ply of the world shuttles is so clamorous and confused, when the labor of the individual is lost in the complexities of production, the old human hand, the symbol of the race, may still be discerned, blurred by the speed of its movements, but master and guide of all that whirring loom.

Study the hand, and you shall find in it the true picture of man, the story of human growth, the measure of the world's greatness and weakness. Its courage, its steadfastness, its pertinacity, make all the welfare of the human race. Upon the trustworthiness of strong, toil-hardened hands rests the life of each and all. Every day thousands of people enter the railway train and trust their lives to the hand that grasps the throttle of the locomotive. Such responsibility kindles the imagination! But more profound is the thought that the destiny and the daily life of mankind depend upon countless obscure hands that are never lifted up in any dramatic gesture to remind the world of their existence. In *Sartor Resartus* Carlyle expresses our obligation to the uncelebrated hands of the worker:

> Venerable to me is the hard Hand; crooked and coarse; wherein notwithstanding lies a cunning virtue indefeasibly royal as the Scepter of this Planet. Hardly entreated Brother! For us was thy

way so bent, for us were thy straight limb and fingers so deformed; thou wert our Conscript on whom the lot fell, and fighting our battles wert so marred. For in thee too lay a God-created Form, but it was not to be unfolded. Encrusted must it stand with the thick adhesions and defacements of Labor; and thy body, like thy soul, was not to know Freedom.

But wherefore these deformities and defacements? Wherefore this bondage that cramps the soul? A million tool-hands are at our service, tireless and efficient, having neither heart nor nerve. Why do they not lift the burden from those bowed shoulders? Can it be that man is captive to his own machine, manacled to his own handiwork, like the convict chained to the prison wall that he himself has built? Instruments multiply, they incorporate more and more of the intelligence of men; they not only perform coarse drudgery, but also imitate accurately many of the hand's most difficult dexterities. Still the God-created Form is bowed. Innumerable souls are still denied their freedom. Still the fighter of our battles is maimed and defrauded.

Once I rejoiced when I heard of a new invention for the comfort of man. Taught by religion and a gentle home life, nourished with good books, I could not but believe that all men had access to the benefits of inventive genius. When I heard that locomotives had doubled in size and speed, I thought: "The food of the wheat fields will come cheaper to the poor of the cities now," and I was glad. But flour costs more today than when I read of those great new engines. Why do not improved methods of milling and trans-portation improve the dinner of the poor? I supposed that in our civilization all advances benefited every man. I imagined that every worthy endeavor brought a sure reward. I had felt in my life the touch only of hands that uphold the weak, hands that are all eye and ear, charged with helpful intelligence. I believed that people made their own conditions, and that if the conditions were not always of the best they were at least tolerable, just as my infirmity was tolerable.

As the years went by, and I read more widely, I learned that the miseries and failures of the poor are not always due to their own faults, that multitudes of men, for some strange reason, fail to share in the much talked of progress of the world. I shall never forget the pain and amazement which I felt when I came to examine the statistics of blindness, its causes and its connections with other calamities that befall thousands of my fellow men. I learned how workmen are stricken by the machine hands that they are operating. It became clear to me that the laborsaving machine does not save the laborer. It saves expense and makes profits for the owner of the machine. The worker has no share in the increased production due to improved methods; and, what is worse, as the eagle was killed by the arrow winged with his own feather, so the hand of the world is wounded by its own skill. The multipotent machine displaces the very hand that created it. The productivity of the machine seems to be valued above the human hand; for the machine is often left without proper safeguards, and so hurts the very life it was intended to serve.

Step by step my investigation of blindness led me into the industrial world. And what a world it is! How different from the world of my beliefs! I must face unflinchingly a world of facts — a world of misery and degradation, of blindness, crookedness and sin, a world struggling against the elements, against the unknown, against itself. How to reconcile this world of fact with the bright world of my imagining? My darkness had been filled with the light of intelligence and, behold, the outer day lit world was stumbling and groping in social blindness! At first I was most unhappy; but deeper study restored my confidence. By learning the sufferings and burdens of men, I became aware as never before of the life power that survived the forces of darkness, the power which, though never completely victorious, is continuously conquering. The very fact that we are still here carrying on the contest against the hosts of annihilation proves that on the whole the battle has gone for humanity. The world's great heart has proved equal to the prodigious undertaking which God set it. Rebuffed, but always persevering; self-reproached, but ever regaining faith; undaunted, tenacious, the heart of man labors toward immeasurably distant goals. Discouraged not by difficulties without or the anguish of ages within, the heart listens to a secret voice that whispers: "Be not dismayed; in the future lies the Promised Land."

When I think of all the wonders that the hand of man has wrought, I rejoice and am lifted up. It seems the image and agent of the Hand that upholds us all. We are its creatures... its triumphs, remade by it in the ages since the birth of the race. Nothing on earth is so thrilling, so terrifying, as the power of our hands to keep us or mar us. All that man does is the hand alive, the hand manifest, creating and destroying, itself the interest of order and demolition. It moves a stone, and the universe undergoes a readjustment. It breaks a clod, and a new beauty bursts forth in fruits and flowers, and the sea of fertility flows over the desert.

With our hands we raise each other to the heights of knowledge and achievement, and with the same hands we plunge each other into the pit. I have stood beside a gun which they told me could in a few minutes destroy a town and the people in it. When I learned how much the gun cost, I thought: "Enough labor is wasted on that gun to build a town full of clean streets and wholesome dwellings!" Misguided hands that destroy their own handiwork and deface the image of God! Wonderful hands that wound and can bind up, that make sore and can heal, suffering all injuries, yet triumphant in measureless enterprise! What on earth is like unto the hands in their possibilities of good and evil? So much creative power has God deputed to us that we can fashion human beings round about with strong sinews and noble limbs, or we can shrivel them up, grind living hearts and living hands in the mills of penury. This power gives me confidence. But because it is often misdirected, my confidence is mingled with discontent.

"Why is it," I asked, and turned to the literature of our day for answer, "why is it that so many workers live in unspeakable misery?" With their hands they have built great cities, and they cannot be sure of a roof over their heads. With their hands they have opened mines and dragged forth with the strength of their bodies the buried sunshine of dead forests, and they are cold. They have gone down into the bowels of the earth for diamonds and gold, and they haggle for a loaf of bread. With their hands they erect temple and palace, and their habitation is a crowded room in a tenement. They plow and sow and fill our hands with flowers while their own hands are full of husks.

In our mills, factories and mines, human hands are herded together to dig, to spin and to feed the machines that they have made, and the product of the machine is not theirs. Day after day naked hands, without safeguard, without respite, must guide the machines under dangerous and unclean conditions. Day after day they must keep firm hold of the little that they grasp of life, until they are hardened, brutalized. Still the portent of idle hands grows apace, and the hand-to-hand grapple waxes more fierce. Oh pitiful blindness! Oh folly that men should allow such contradictions — contradictions that violate not only the higher justice, but the plainest common sense. How do the hands that have achieved the Mauretania become so impotent that they cannot save themselves from drowning? How do our hands that have stretched railways and telegraphs round the world become so shortened that they cannot redeem themselves?

Why is it that willing hands are denied the prerogatives of labor, that the hand of man is against man? At the bidding of a single hand thousands rush to produce, or hang idle. Amazing that hands which produce nothing should be exalted and jewelled with authority! In yonder town the textile mills are idle, and the people want shoes. Fifty miles away, in another town, the shoe factories are silent, and the people want clothes. Between these two arrested forces of production is that record of profits and losses called *the market.* The buyers of clothes and shoes in the market are the workers themselves; but they cannot buy what their hands have made. Is it not unjust that the hands of the world are not subject to the will of the workers, but are driven by the blind force of necessity to obey the will of the few? And who are these few? They are themselves the slaves of the market and the victims of necessity.

Driven by the very maladjustments that wound it, and enabled by its proved capacity for readjustment and harmony, society must move onward to a state in which every hand shall work and reap the fruits of its own endeavor, no less, no more. This is the third world which I have discovered. From a world of dreams I was plunged into a world of fact, and thence I have emerged into a society which is still a dream, but rooted in the actual. The commonwealth of the future is growing surely out of the state in which we now live. There will be strife, but no aimless, self-defeating strife. There will be competition, but no soul destroying, hand crippling competition. There will be only honest emulation in cooperative effort. There will be example to instruct, companionship to cheer and to lighten burdens. Each hand will do its part in the provision of food, clothing, shelter and the other great needs of man, so that if poverty comes all will bear it alike, and if prosperity shines all will rejoice in its warmth.

There have been such periods in the history of man. Human nature has proved itself capable of equal cooperation. But the early communist societies, of which history tells us, were primitive in their methods of production — half civilized, as we say who dare call our present modes of life civilization. The coming age will be complex, and will relinquish nothing useful in the methods which it has learned in long struggles through tyrannies and fierce rivalries of possession. To the hand of the world belongs the best, the noblest, the most stupendous task, the subjection of all the forces of nature to the mind of man, the subjection of physical strength to the might of the spirit. We are still far from this loftiest of triumphs of the hand. Its forces are still to be disciplined and organized. The limbs of the world must first be restored. In order that no limb may suffer, and that none may keep the others in bondage, the will of the many must become self-conscious and intelligently united. Then the hand — the living power of man, the hewer of the world — will be laid with undisputed sway upon the machine with which it has so long been confounded. There will be abundance for all, and no hands will cry out any more against the arm of the might. The hand of the world will then have achieved what it now obscurely symbolizes: The uplifting and regeneration of the race, all that is highest, all that is creative in man.

# Letter to Helen Keller from Muriel Symington
(1955)

Dear Miss Keller:

I feel it to be quite inappropriate to felicitate you on your 75th birthday but rather that we should congratulate ourselves for the privilege of living during your time — to be sustained and inspired by the full, rich life you have led and, pray heaven, that you will be leading for years to come...

I felt very close to your life and work last fall when my dear friend, Elizabeth Gurley Flynn, granted me the privilege of typing her autobiography — the first volume from the outset of her career to the tragic conclusion of the Sacco and Vanzetti case. During the chronicle of those crowded years — fruitful fighting on many fronts — your name and the names of many other distinguished Americans crop up many times. But none of them elicited from her pen greater affection and respect than she exhibited for you.

Elizabeth is now in her sixth month of imprisonment at the Federal Women's Reformatory, Alderson, West Virginia, and I in common with a multitude of other friends and admirers, count the days until her three year sentence — less time off for good behavior — comes to an end. While nothing can lessen my deep indignation over this barbarity, my sense of loss is mitigated somewhat for my friend conferred on me a wholly undeserved distinction in requesting that I might be one of her permitted correspondents, and I was accepted. The rules are very strict and I am not permitted to quote any passages from her beautiful letters to me. At moments when my spirits flag, the serene fortitude shining through what she writes is a great solace, leaving me at the same time ashamed that it is the one in prison who sets me an example of unfaltering and unselfconscious courage.

Miss Keller, Elizabeth's 65th birthday falls on August 7 and I can think of nothing that would give her more joy than to receive a card with a message from you. Ordinarily such greetings, unless from accepted correspondents are not delivered, but only turned over to the prisoner on release. But I have a feeling that a card and message bearing your name would be made an exception to the rule...

Please accept my greeting of affection and profound admiration.
Muriel I. Symington

# Help Soviet Russia
The *Toiler* (1921)

I love Russia and all who stand loyally by her in her mighty wrestlings with the giant powers of ignorance and imperialist greed. When I first heard of the glorious words, "Soviet Republic of Russia," it was as if a new light shone through my darkness. I felt that the sun of a better day had risen upon the world. Those glowing, hope inspiring words, "Soviet Republic of Russia," meant that at last the principles of truth, justice and brotherhood had gained a foothold upon earth, and this thought has run like a shining furrow through the dark years that have intervened. We have witnessed Russia's superhuman struggle in a world blinded by avarice and calumny. But despite intrigues and blockades and the wicked misinterpretations of a stupid, dishonest press, she stands today firmly entrenched in her just cause, while the old social order is collapsing at her feet.

Oh, why cannot the workers see that the cause of Russia is their cause? Her struggle for economic freedom is their struggle, her perishing children are their children, and her dreams, her aspirations, her martyrdom and victories are an internal part of the workers' campaign for a better, saner world. Why can they not understand that their own best instincts are in revolt against a social order which enthralls masses of men and leads inevitably to poverty, suffering and war? How spiritually blind are men, that they fail to see that we are all bound together! We rise or fall together, we are dwarfed or godlike, free or chained together.

If the workers would only use their minds a little, instead of letting others do their thinking for them, they would see quickly through the flimsy arguments of the newspapers they read. They are told that the famine in Russia is caused by "Marxian socialism," and that four years of Bolshevism have brought Russia to the doors of the world begging for bread. If that is true, what has caused the famine in China? What is the cause of undernourishment in some of our southern states? And what is the cause of unemployment throughout this great, rich land? Begging for bread is not uncommon within the capitalistic nations, and these days we hear a great deal of soup kitchens and the bread line. These phenomena occur even in times which the newspapers are accustomed to speak of as "prosperous."

The famine in Russia is the result of a drought following years of war and a long imperialistic blockade of Russian ports, preventing entrance to them of all necessary supplies. This is the plain truth. Yet millions of sensible men and women have been deceived about conditions in Russia. But I trust that the good sense of the American people will soon surmount the wall of calumnies and prejudices which now prevents friendly relations between the two countries.

Through the mist of tears and sweat and blood of struggling men I salute her and wish for her the love of an awakened and grateful humanity.

Here is a thought that keeps singing in my mind but will not fold its wings for the formal limits of a letter:

Great, O Russia, is thy task! Thine is the race immortal whose beams shall spread across the earth, wide as the wings of heaven, bright as the morning light. Lift high thy flaming torch wherever men are slaves! Breathe upon them the life quickening fires of thy creative mind. Give them the potent red light of thy courage, that they may look upon the faces of comrades in every land, and be to all their kind dear friends and neighbors. Then shall all men discover thee, a paradise upon the verge of doom.

# part three: Women

## To an English Woman Suffragist
Manchester *Advertiser* (1911)

I thank you for the copy of *Votes for Women*. Mr. Zangwill's address interested me deeply. You ask me to comment on it, and though I know little, your request encourages me to tell you some of my ideas on the subject.

I have thought much lately about the question of women's suffrage, and I have followed in my Braille magazines the recent elections in Great Britain. The other day I read a fine report of an address by Miss Pankhurst at a meeting in New York.

I do not believe that the present government has any intention of giving women a part in national politics, or doing justice to Ireland, or the workmen of England. So long as the franchise is denied to a large number of those who serve and benefit the public, so long as those who vote are at the beck and call of party machines, the people are not free, and the day of women's freedom seems still to be in the far future. It makes no difference whether the Tories or the Liberals in Great Britain, the Democrats or the Republicans in the United States, or any party of the old model in any other country, get the upper hand. To ask any such party for women's rights is like asking a czar for democracy.

Are not the dominant parties managed by the ruling classes, that is, the propertied classes, solely for the profit and privilege of the few? They use us millions to help them into power. They tell us, like so many children, that our safety lies in voting for them. They toss us crumbs of concession to make us believe that they are working in our interest. Then they exploit the resources of the nation not for us, but for the interests which they represent and uphold. We, the people, are not free. Our democracy is but a name. We vote? What does that mean? It means that we choose between two bodies of real, though not avowed, autocrats. We choose between Tweedledum and Tweedledee. We elect expensive masters to do our work for us, and then blame them because they work for themselves and for their class.

The enfranchisement of women is a part of the vast movement to enfranchise all mankind. You ask for votes for women. What good can votes do you when ten-elevenths of the land of Great Britain belongs to 200,000, and only one-eleventh to the rest of the 40 million? Have your men with their millions of votes freed themselves from this injustice?

When one shows the masters that half the wealth of Great Britain belongs to 25,000 persons, when one says that this is wrong, that this wrong lies at the bottom of all social injustice, including the wrong of women, the highly respectable newspapers cry "Socialist Agitator! Stirrer of Class Strife!" Well, let us agitate; let us confess that we are thoroughgoing Social Democrats, or anything else that they please to label us. But let us keep our eyes on the central fact that a few, a few British men own the majority of British men and all British women. The few own the many, because they possess the means of livelihood of all. In our splendid republic, where at election time all are free and equal, a few Americans own the rest. Eighty percent of our people live in rented houses, and one-half of the rest are mortgaged.

The country is governed for the richest, for the corporations, the bankers, the land speculators and for the exploiters of labor. Surely we must free men and women together before we can free women.

The majority of mankind are working people. So long as their fair demands — the ownership and control of their lives and livelihood — are set at naught, we can have neither men's rights nor women's rights. The majority of mankind is ground down by industrial oppression in order that the small remnant may live in ease. How can women hope to help themselves while we and our brothers are helpless against the powerful organizations which modern parties represent and which contrive to rule the people. They rule the people because they own the means of physical life, land and tools, and the nourishers. Of intellectual life, the press, the church and the school.

You say that the conduct of the women suffragists is being disgracefully misrepresented by the British press. Here in America the leading newspapers misrepresent in every possible way the struggles of toiling men and women who seek relief. News that reflects ill upon the employers is skillfully concealed; news of dreadful conditions under which laborers are forced to produce; news of thousands of men maimed in mills and mines and left without compensation; news of famines and strikes; news of thousands of women driven to a life of shame; news of little children compelled to labor before their hands are ready to drop their toys. Only here and there in a small and as yet uninfluential paper is the truth told about the workman and the fearful burdens under which he staggers.

I am indignant at the treatment of the brave, patient women of England. I am indignant when the women cloakmakers of Chicago are abused by the police. I am filled with anguish when I think of the degradation, the enslavement and the industrial tyranny which crushes millions and drags down women and helpless children.

I know the deep interest which you and your husband always

took in God's poor, and your sympathy invites me to open my heart to you and express these opinions about grave problems.

# Why Men Need Woman Suffrage

New York *Call* (1913)

Many declare that the woman peril is at our door. I have no doubt that it is. Indeed, I suspect that it has already entered most households. Certainly a great number of men are facing it across the breakfast table. And no matter how deaf they pretend to be, they cannot help hearing it talk.

Women insist on their "divine rights," "immutable rights," "inalienable rights." These phrases are not so sensible as one might wish. When one comes to think of it, there are no such things as divine, immutable or inalienable rights. Rights are things we get when we are strong enough to make good our claim to them. Men spent hundreds of years and did much hard fighting to get the rights they now call divine, immutable and inalienable. Today women are demanding rights that tomorrow nobody will be foolhardy enough to question. Anyone that reads intelligently knows that some of our old ideas are up a tree, and that traditions are scurrying away before the advance of their everlasting enemy, the questioning mind of a new age. It is time to take a good look at human affairs in the light of new conditions and new ideas, and the tradition that man is the natural master of the destiny of the race is one of the first to suffer investigation.

The dullest can see that a good many things are wrong with the world. It is old-fashioned, running into ruts. We lack intelligent direction and control. We are not getting the most out of our opportunities and advantages. We must make over the scheme of life, and new tools are needed for the work. Perhaps one of the chief reasons for the present chaotic condition of things is that the world has been trying to get along with only half of itself. Everywhere we see running to waste woman-force that should be utilized in making the world a more decent home for humanity. Let us see how the votes of women will help solve the problem of living wisely and well.

When women vote men will no longer be compelled to guess at their desires — and guess wrong. Women will be able to protect themselves from man-made laws that are antagonistic to their interests. Some persons like to imagine that man's chivalrous nature will constrain him to act humanely toward woman and protect her rights. Some men do protect some women. We demand that all women have the right to protect themselves and relieve man of this feudal responsibility.

Political power shapes the affairs of state and determines many of the everyday relations of human beings with one another. The citizen with a vote is master of his own destiny. Women without this power, and who do not happen to have "natural protectors," are at the mercy of man-made laws. And experience shows that these laws are often unjust to them. Legislation made to protect women who have fathers and husbands to care for them does not protect working women whose only defenders are the state's policemen.

The wages of women in some states belong to their fathers or their husbands. They cannot hold property. In parts of this enlightened democracy of men the father is the sole owner of the child. I believe he can even will away the unborn babies. Legislation concerning the age of consent is another proof that the voice of woman is mute in the halls of the lawmakers. The regulations affecting laboring women are a proof that men are too busy to protect their "natural wards."

Economic urgencies have driven women to demand the vote. To a large number of women is entrusted the vitally important public function of training all children. Yet it is frequently impossible for teachers to support themselves decently on their wages. What redress have these overworked, underpaid women without the vote? They count for nothing politically.

An organization of women recently wanted to obtain a welfare measure from a legislature in New York. A petition signed by 5,000 women was placed before the chairman of a committee that was to report on the bill. He said it was a good bill and ought to pass. After the women had waited a reasonable time, they sent up a request to know what had become of the bill. The chairman said he did not know anything about it. He was reminded of the petition that had been brought to him signed by 5,000 women. "Oh," replied the chairman, "a petition signed by 5,000 women is not worth the paper it is written on. Get five men to sign and we'll do something about it." That is one reason we demand the vote — we want 5,000 women to count for more than five men.

A majority of women that need the vote are wage earners. A tremendous change has taken place in the industrial world since power machines took the place of hand tools. Men and women have been compelled to adjust themselves to a new system of production and distribution. The machine has been used to exploit the labor of both men and women as it was never exploited before. In the terrific struggle for existence that has resulted from this change women and children suffer even more than men. Indeed, economic pressure drives many women to market their sex.

Yet women have nothing to say about conditions under which they live and toil. Helpless, unheeded, they must endure hardships that lead to misery and degradation. They may not lift a hand to defend themselves against cruel, crippling processes that stunt the body and brain and bring on early death or premature old age.

Workingmen suffer from the helplessness of working women. They must compete in the same offices and factories with women who are unable to protect themselves with proper laws. They must compete with women who work in unsanitary rooms called homes, work by dim lamps in the night, rocking a cradle with one foot. It is to the interest of all workers to end this stupid, one-sided, one power arrangement and have suffrage for all.

The laws made by men rule the minds as well as the bodies of women. The man-managed state so conducts its schools that the ideals of women are warped to hideous shapes. Governments and schools engender and nourish a militant public opinion that makes war always possible. Man-written history, fiction and poetry glorify war. Love of country is turned into patriotism which suggests drums, flags and young men eager to give their lives to the rulers of the nation. There will continue to be wars so long as our schools make such ideas prevail.

Women know the cost of human life in terms of suffering and sacrifice as men can never know it. I believe women would use the ballot to prevent war and to destroy the ideas that make war possible. In spite of an education that has taught them to glorify the military element in their ideals of manhood, they will wake to the realization that he loves his country best who lives for it and serves it faithfully. They will teach children to honor the heroes of peace above the heroes of war.

Women are even now more active in working for social legislation and laws affecting the schools, the milk supply and the quality of food than are the men who have the votes. Fundamentally, woman is a more social being than man. She is concerned with the whole family, while man is more individualistic. Social consciousness is not so strong in him. Many questions can be solved only with the help of woman's social experience — questions of the safety of women in their work, the rights of little children.

Yet her peculiar knowledge and abilities are made the basis of arguments against giving women the vote. It is indisputably true that woman is constituted for the purposes of maternity. So is man constituted for the purposes of paternity. But no-one seems to think that incapacitates him for citizenship. If there is a fundamental difference between man and woman, far be it from me to deny that it exists. It is all the more reason why her side should be heard.

For my part, I should think that man's chivalrous nature would cause him to emancipate the weaker half of the race. Indeed, is seems strange that when he was getting the suffrage for himself it did not occur to him to divide up with his beloved partner. Looking closer, I almost detect a suspicion of tyranny in his attitude toward her on the suffrage question. And can it be that this tyranny wears the mask of chivalry? Please do not misunderstand me. I am not disparaging chivalry. It is a very fine thing — what there is of it. The trouble is, there is not enough to go around. Nearly all the opportunities, educational and political, that woman has acquired have been gained by a march of conquest with a skirmish at every post.

So since masculine chivalry has failed us we must hustle a bit and see what we can do for ourselves — and the men who need our suffrage. First of all, we must organize. We must make ourselves so aggressive a political factor that our natural protectors can no longer deny us a voice in directing and shaping the laws under which we must live.

We shall not see the end of capitalism and the triumph of democracy until men and women work together in the solving of their political, social and economic problems. I realize that the vote is only one of many weapons in our fight for the freedom of all. But every means is precious and, equipped with the vote, men and women together will hasten the day when the age-long dream of liberty, equality and brotherhood shall be realized upon earth.

# The New Woman's Party
New York *Call* (1916)

For the first time in the history of America women have become a great factor in the selection of a presidential candidate and the creation of a party's platform. They are seen everywhere in Chicago in these convention discussions, where a very few years ago their appearance would have caused untold comment. And their influence is affecting every "deal" that the politicians are making. Greatest of all they have just formed a "Woman's Party," the birth of which I saw as it started winging its way down the ages.

What does all this mean?

What message does this hold for the women of America, of the world?

The Woman's Party means more than votes for women. It is the symbol of our solidarity. It stands for the best national efforts of American women. It embodies the aspirations of millions of intelligent women — women who think and have enlightened opinions. It focuses our struggle for independence.

The Woman's Party stands for Woman First. It means an individual allegiance to our ideal — the ideal of sex equality and responsibility.

It means more and more united, effective cooperation.

Women have discovered that they cannot rely on man's chivalry to give them justice — just as men before them found out that we cannot be saved by other people — we must save ourselves.

Man has fought hard for the extension of his franchise; it has sometimes caused bloodshed. Today women are met with the same arguments that were used against the political emancipation of men. It was argued by the masters that the propertyless mob was not competent to vote; that they did not want the vote;

that only a few noisy demagogues were stirring the people and filling their heads with foolishness. The idea that they were capable of taking intelligent interest in political questions was ridiculed.

But no ridicule, no argument, no force could daunt those who fought for manhood suffrage.

The justice of our cause is as obvious, as compelling, as theirs. Our need to take part in controlling the affairs of the world is imperative. The love of power is strong in the human breast, and men, having once secured their suffrage, will keep it for themselves until we force them to extend it to women.

The time is ripe for us; there are now four million women voters in the United States. The party that turns them down is dead politically. Of course, our victory is not won; we shall have to work long and endure much before our dreams are realized. But the new Woman's Party will give the two old parties a jolt at the presidential election that will set them thinking and acting.

At every stage of history there comes a moment when decisive action brings all the struggles of the past into realization. This is one of those moments in the nation's life and in the life of women.

# Great American Women
The Heroic Careers of Three Famous Champions of Women's Rights
*Home* magazine (1932)

I hold in my heart the memory of three loving and courageous women — women who possessed a gracious presence, unusual intelligence and great eloquence. They listened to the "voices" in their youth, like Joan of Arc, and their demands kept Susan B. Anthony, Lucy Stone and Elizabeth Cady Stanton young and beautiful even into old age.

Elizabeth Cady Stanton was born in Seneca Falls, New York, in 1815, and lived to see the century out. Her father was a Supreme Court judge. At the age of 25 she married Mr. Henry Brewster Stanton, a descendant of the Puritan elder. She was not dazzled by this distinction, nor was she much impressed by Puritanism. But Mr. Stanton was a leading abolitionist, and was sent as a delegate to the World's Antislavery Convention which met in London in 1840.

Elizabeth was a girl of high spirit, eager to see the world. She married on Friday (the word "obey" was omitted from the ceremony), and on Monday she sailed for England. On this eventful journey she met Lucretia Mott, and shared with her the humiliation of being excluded from the Antislavery Convention floor on account of her sex — an act of tactlessness to which we probably owe the Anglo-American movement for women's political equality.

A convention called by Mrs. Stanton and Lucretia Mott in Seneca Falls, 1848, placed her name on the revolutionary roll call. Not long afterwards she joined Susan B. Anthony and a few kindred spirits to form the first women's rights organization in this country. This was the beginning of the lifelong struggle of these women against repressive laws and traditions affecting women.

Their "wants" were so numerous, just to name them would fill my space! I will mention a few of them. They wanted bloomers, they wanted divorce, they wanted the franchise, they wanted equal pay, they wanted to enter the professions on equal terms with men, they wanted education. They stopped at nothing until the Civil War came along and put an end to their "unseemly practice of public lectures" throughout the country.

Susan B. Anthony was born in South Adams, Massachusetts. Her environment molded her for the destiny she was to fulfill. She had experience as a teacher and a factory worker. The hard life her mother and neighbors lived kindled in her the flame of the crusader.

She became interested in temperance work. To her surprise and indignation she was denied admission to a meeting of temperance workers because she was a woman.

She was present at the convention called by Mrs. Stanton and Lucretia Mott at Seneca Falls. Mrs. Stanton and Miss Anthony seem to have been created for each other, and certainly they were as one in every crisis of their heroic lives. Miss Anthony also met Lucy Stone at the Seneca Falls convention for the first time.

Lucy Stone was born in 1818, on a picturesque, rocky farm near West Brookfield, Massachusetts. Her mother, a farmer's wife, had milked eight cows the night before Lucy was born, as a sudden shower had obliged all the men of the family to rush to the fields and save the hay. When she was told the sex of the new baby (the eighth of nine children), the mother immediately cried, "Oh, dear, I am so sorry it's a girl. A woman's life is so hard!" I like to think that the baby born of that weary, sad mother was destined to make life less hard for all the generations of women that were to follow.

The world upon which Lucy's bright eyes opened was very different from the world of our day. Women were not admitted to the colleges. No free high school for girls existed. It was generally believed that a woman should receive only enough instruction to enable her to read the Psalms and to keep her household accounts, and that any attempt to give her more knowledge would ruin her as a wife and mother.

Public speaking for women was taboo. Even to write for publication was considered unwomanly. Law, religion and custom affirmed the inferiority of women.

Lucy Stone was the first married woman in America to keep her own name. She was also the first woman to receive a college degree. She converted Susan B. Anthony and Julia Ward Howe to the Suffragists' cause. She was the founder and editor of *The Woman's Journal* in Boston, which was the principal woman suffrage newspaper of the United States for nearly half a century. During their heroic careers these three women champions of women's rights, revealed the qualities of steadfastness, independent thinking and large sympathy.

We of today can have little conception of the difficulties these women encountered, or the brutal prejudice that pursued them ceaselessly. They were accused of being infidels and atheists! They were charged with being free lovers! It was asserted and reiterated that they were bent upon undermining the sacredness of the institution of marriage, breaking up the family and destroying the home! Yet the cause for which those women were slandered is triumphant today.


# Put Your Husband in the Kitchen
*Atlantic Monthly* (1932)

...Our grandmothers had to perform a tremendous amount of dreary drudgery in managing their homes. They were kept busy from morning till night, for those were the days when a woman's work was never done. Since then, however, the machine age has come upon us, transforming the home no less surely than the factory. The housewife of today finds that many heavy responsibilities which she would have had to assume in any other age, such as the baking of bread and the weaving of the cloth, have been lifted from her, and scores of other tasks which still remain in her province have been so simplified that they can now be performed with a great saving of time and effort. Electricity and gas and innumerable mechanical devices have reduced household labor to a fraction of its former burden. In consequence, the modern woman enjoys a degree of leisure which her grandmother could hardly have dared to dream of.

Whether women are using their new found leisure to its full advantage is a debatable question, and one which I shall not attempt to discuss here. The point that I want to emphasize is that they have it — and they have it because of these countless machines and clever contrivances which have been invented to save time and labor.

This, of course, is a very familiar observation, and I claim no credit for originality in mentioning it. But recently, as I was turning over in my mind the tragic muddle of present economic conditions, it suddenly occurred to me that this commonplace is not nearly as hackneyed as it may seem. Few of us seemed to have grasped the significance of this new leisureliness which has come to grace our households. As a matter of plain fact, what women have done with labor-saving machinery in the home is exactly the reverse of what men have done with it in their factories and offices. The captain of industry seizes upon improved tools as means to increase production, and now he finds the channels of trade clogged with more goods than can be sold; his wife uses them to produce leisure, of which she can never have too much.

The average woman is not very familiar with the complexities of economics, but it seems that she has ordered her household economy upon a more solid basis than that upon which men have arranged the affairs of their larger world. In industry, the amazing increase in the use of labor-saving machinery has brought about overproduction, unemployment and widespread suffering. Either women are wiser, or they have a sounder instinct for economics. At any rate, they use labor-saving devices for the heretical purpose of saving labor, and in doing so they have, I think, demonstrated in their homes a practical object lesson in economics which their husbands would do well to master. While theorists are still searching for the causes of the depression, and politicians remain at loggerheads in their effort to conjure remedies, I am tempted to think that the perplexed businessman might discover a possible solution to his troubles if he would just spend a few days in his wife's kitchen.

Let us see what would happen if he did.

Mr. Jones, let us say, is a modern captain of industry. Mrs. Jones is an intelligent woman who knows more than the average person about economics, and has the knack of seeing things through to their essentials. She had often discussed business problems with her husband, and had endeavored without success to win him to her point of view. At last she decided to try an experiment. She persuaded her husband that he owed it to humanity to demonstrate the correctness of his ideas by applying them to the home — the one field which men had not yet touched with their organizing genius. Mr. Jones accepted the challenge and agreed to serve for a term as cook, maid and household manager. He promised to see what improvements he could effect by directing all domestic activities in precisely the same way that he conducted his own business.

Mr. Jones had grown up on a farm. The chores that fell to his lot as a boy made him familiar with the drudgery of household work in former days. Although he was vaguely aware that the home had kept pace with the mechanical age, he did not know what a startling revolution had taken place in the economy of the household until he surveyed his wife's model kitchen, with its gas range, its dishwashing machine, its electric mixer and its various other labor-saving appliances. He investigated the interior of the compact kitchen cabinet, containing all sorts of prepared foods. He was particularly impressed by the special cake flour and the shelled nuts.

"Ah, the wonders of science and modern efficiency!" he said to himself. "I remember the fine nut cakes my mother used to make. What a job it was in those days! But now, with all these prepared ingredients, with the electric mixer and the automatically regulated gas range, I ought to be able to make 10 cakes in less time and with less trouble than my mother required to make one in her primitive household."

So, true to the ideas which had made him captain of the industry, Mr. Jones proceeded to transform potential power into actuality. When the family assembled at the dinner table that evening, the new household manager could hardly restrain his enthusiasm. Laughingly, he said to his wife: "See now, Mary, what I have done. Ten cakes. Ten! When you were running the house we had only one, or two at most. Ah, the logical, orderly, efficient brain of a man is needed even in the kitchen, that sacred province of woman. In one day I have revolutionized the business of cooking, and have put it on a sound basis."

The cakes were good, and the family ate almost a whole one with relish. They were persuaded to finish it. But there were still nine left. By good salesmanship the industrialist-turned-cook induced the family to eat another, which they did to please him, but they had no relish for it. At this point Mr. Jones found himself confronted with the same problem which he had to face every day in his business — he would have to sell more. Inventory could have been reduced, unit costs slashed. That could be done only stimulating demand and increasing consumption. So he employed the cash rebate system, offering small William a dime to place his order for a large section of the third cake. William saw that it was a consumer market; he knew that such wonders are natural and impermanent, and could not resist stocking up. In the end, by using every known trick of the salesman's art, Mr. Jones coaxed, wheedled and bribed the family to dispose of the third cake. By this time everybody had arrived at a stage of acute discomfort and complete indifference to his further entreaties, and he recognized the symptoms of a saturated market.

That night the family physician was kept busy ministering to varying degrees of indigestion from mild to acute. The care with which Mr. Jones had nurtured the family put them in good stead, however, and all were fairly well recovered by morning.

At breakfast Mrs. Jones said to her husband: "Of course you realize that the doctor's fees will have to come out of your budget. It was all your fault."

"But I have no reserves set aside for that," replied Mr. Jones. "You know that before we changed places I always paid the doctor. His bill shouldn't be charged against the household budget."

"Just the same," said Mrs. Jones "I'm afraid you'll have to add it to your production costs. Then next time you'll know better that to glut the market."

For once Mr. Jones had nothing to say, and his wife continued: "Fortunately, we shall not want any more cake for a long time to come. But when we do, you can bake ten, if you must, and then throw away nine. You can't object to that. I understand that such methods are common in your economic world. "Maintaining the market" — isn't that what you call it? It won't be the first time food has been destroyed to maintain the market. And, of course, you manufacturers are constantly producing goods that go to waste because of lack of demand. So I shouldn't dare suggest that you bake only one cake merely because that is all we need. That would be heresy. It would be inefficient. It would be criminal failure to take advantage of "plant capacity." The gas stove will easily hold 10 cakes, and the same gas that will bake one will bake the others too. The electric mixer also represents an investment. You should not let it stand idle, for the overhead will ruin us. So go ahead with your plans, John. I just know you are going to do remarkable things in increasing production and cutting unit costs — but don't forget to dispose of your surplus.".....

No-one, of course, would act as foolishly in the realm of household economics as did this mythical Mr. Jones, but there are many Mr. Joneses who have acted no less foolishly in their own sphere of large-scale industry, expanding plants and piling up goods with complete disregard for market demand. It may be argued that the parallel I have drawn is not a fair one because the family unit is so small and static that its requirements can be easily gauged, while there is no element of competition in supplying these requirements. But the nation, after all, is only the sum of these small units, and with proper cooperation it should not be impossible to estimate, within certain limits, the amount of goods the nation needs.

Here, of course, arises the question of whether we are at present suffering from overproduction or under consumption — the question, in short, of purchasing power. This is a large subject which I do not have space to deal with in this article, but I hope to write about it some other time. The only point I want to make here is this: that it is about time for us to begin using our labor-saving machinery actually to save labor instead of using it to flood the nation haphazardly with surplus goods which clog the channels of trade. That will presuppose, to be sure, some cooperative effort to determine the needs of the people and to produce accordingly.

In the allegory of Mr. Jones, perhaps Mrs. Jones came off better than she should. She has obtained leisure, certainly, but it is doubtful whether the hundreds of thousands of Mrs. Joneses throughout the land are making the best use of the new wealth of hours which the labor-saving devices in their homes have made possible. But at least the opportunity is there. Women have won the first skirmish, whereas in the industrial world — the world of men — the machine is battering at the very livelihood of our beleaguered people. If we are to win this larger battle, we must adopt a new collective view of the machine and the complex economic structure which has been erected upon it.

I am convinced that the machine has taken something out of life. We have paid, and are still paying a great price for the benefits it has given us. But the fault lies with us. We have not used it properly. If the progress of the mechanical age should suddenly cease now, I should say that its disadvantages had outweighed its benefits. But further developments are certain to come. We cannot now throw the machine overboard. It is with us to stay, and our task is to turn it to our proper need. In the machine, rightly controlled, lies the hope of reducing human drudgery to the minimum — not merely that we may be free of drudgery, but that every individual may have the opportunity for a happy life, for a leisure which, under wise guidance, may lead to mental and spiritual growth.

I do not set myself up as an expert economist, but from my detached position I have tried to examine the whole problem from a humanitarian and commonsense point of view. It is evident to me, as it must be to all thinking people, that the manufacture and exchange of goods constitute the preponderant influences in modern life. That is a false emphasis. Now, at last, we have an opportunity gradually to shift that emphasis by using labor-saving machinery for its ostensible purpose of saving labor. This will mean a reduction in the hours of toil for the great masses of people. The trend is already in that direction, as an emergency measure, and I am convinced that the pressure toward this end will outlast the emergency, for it is a logical result of the flowering of the mechanical age. This new orientation is by no means impossible. If I thought it were, I should lose my faith in humanity.

After all, is it too much to expect that our ingenuity can reorganize our economic system to take advantage of the machines which we have created? It is largely up to the men — the statesmen and the captains of industry; and, if they are unable to accomplish the task, we women shall have to send them into the kitchen for a few lessons in commonsense economics.

[Article slightly abridged]

# part four: War

# Strike Against War

New York *Call* (1916)

To begin with, I have a word to say to my good friends, the editors, and others who are moved to pity me. Some people are grieved because they imagine I am in the hands of unscrupulous persons who lead me astray and persuade me to espouse unpopular causes and make me the mouthpiece of their propaganda. Now, let it be understood once and for all that I do not want their pity; I would not change places with one of them. I know what I am talking about. My sources of information are as good and reliable as anybody else's. I have papers and magazines from England, France, Germany and Austria that I can read myself. Not all the editors I have met can do that. Quite a number of them have to take their French and German second hand. No, I will not disparage the editors. They are an overworked, misunderstood class. Let them remember, though, that if I cannot see the fire at the end of their cigarettes, neither can they thread a needle in the dark. All I ask, gentlemen, is a fair field and no favor. I have entered the fight against preparedness and against the economic system under which we live. It is to be a fight to the finish, and I ask no quarter.

The future of the world rests in the hands of America. The future of America rests on the backs of 80 million workingmen and women and their children. We are facing a grave crisis in our national life. The few who profit from the labor of the masses want to organize the workers into an army which will protect the interests of the capitalists. You are urged to add to the heavy burdens you already bear the burden of a larger army and many additional warships. It is in your power to refuse to carry the artillery and the dreadnoughts and to shake off some of the burdens, too, such as limousines, steam yachts and country estates. You do not need to make a great noise about it. With the silence and dignity of creators you can end wars and the system of selfishness and exploitation that causes wars. All you need to do to bring about this stupendous revolution is to straighten up and fold your arms.

We are not preparing to defend our country. Even if we were as helpless as Congressman Gardner says we are, we have no enemies foolhardy enough to attempt to invade the United States. The talk about attack from Germany and Japan is absurd. Germany has its hands full and will be busy with its own affairs for some generations after the European war is over.

With full control of the Atlantic Ocean and the Mediterranean Sea, the allies failed to land enough men to defeat the Turks at Gallipoli; and then they failed again to land an army at Salonica in time to check the Bulgarian invasion of Serbia. The conquest of America by water is a nightmare confined exclusively to ignorant persons and members of the Navy League. Yet, everywhere, we hear fear advanced as argument for armament. It reminds me of a fable I read. A certain man found a horseshoe. His neighbor began to weep and wail because, as he justly pointed out, the man who found the horseshoe might someday find a horse. Having found the shoe, he might shoe him. The neighbor's child might some day go so near the horse's heels as to be kicked, and die. Undoubtedly the two families would quarrel and fight, and several valuable lives would be lost through the finding of the horseshoe. You know in the last war we quite accidentally picked up some islands in the Pacific Ocean which may some day be the cause of a quarrel between ourselves and Japan. I'd rather drop those islands right now and forget about them than go to war to keep them. Wouldn't you?

Congress is not preparing to defend the people of the United States. It is planning to protect the capital of American speculators and investors in Mexico, South America, China and the Philippine Islands. Incidentally this preparation will benefit the manufacturers of munitions and war machines.

Until recently there were uses in the United States for the money taken from the workers. But American labor is exploited almost to the limit now, and our national resources have all been appropriated. Still the profits keep piling up new capital. Our flourishing industry in implements of murder is filling the vaults of New York's banks with gold. And a dollar that is not being used to make a slave of some human being is not fulfilling its purpose in the capitalistic scheme. That dollar must be invested in South America, Mexico, China or the Philippines.

It was no accident that the Navy League came into prominence at the same time that the National City Bank of New York established a branch in Buenos Aires. It is not a mere coincidence that six business associates of J. P. Morgan are officials of defense leagues. And chance did not dictate that Mayor Mitchel should appoint to his Committee of Safety a thousand men that represent a fifth of the wealth of the United States. These men want their foreign investments protected.

Every modern war has had its root in exploitation. The Civil War was fought to decide whether the slaveholders of the South or the capitalists of the North should exploit the West. The Spanish-American War decided that the United States should exploit Cuba and the Philippines. The South African War decided that the British should exploit the diamond mines. The Russo-

Japanese War decided that Japan should exploit Korea. The present war is to decide who shall exploit the Balkans, Turkey, Persia, Egypt, India, China, Africa. And we are whetting our sword to scare the victors into sharing the spoils with us. Now, the workers are not interested in the spoils; they will not get any of them anyway.

The preparedness propagandists have still another object, and a very important one. They want to give the people something to think about besides their own unhappy condition. They know the cost of living is high, wages are low, employment is uncertain and will be much more so when the European call for munitions stops. No matter how hard and incessantly the people work, they often cannot afford the comforts of life; many cannot obtain the necessities.

Every few days we are given a new war scare to lend realism to their propaganda. They have had us on the verge of war over the *Lusitania,* the *Gulflight,* the *Ancona,* and now they want the workingmen to become excited over the sinking of the *Persia.* The workingman has no interest in any of these ships. The Germans might sink every vessel on the Atlantic Ocean and the Mediterranean Sea, and kill Americans with every one. The American workingman would still have no reason to go to war. All the machinery of the system has been set in motion. Above the complaint and din of the protest from the workers is heard the voice of authority.

"Friends," it says, "fellow workmen, patriots; your country is in danger! There are foes on all sides of us. There is nothing between us and our enemies except the Pacific Ocean and the Atlantic Ocean. Look at what has happened to Belgium. Consider the fate of Serbia. Will you murmur about low wages when your country, your very liberties, are in jeopardy? What are the miseries you endure compared to the humiliation of having a victorious German Army sail up the East River? Quit your whining, get busy and prepare to defend your firesides and your flag. Get an army, get a navy; be ready to meet the invaders like the loyal hearted free men you are."

Will the workers walk into this trap? Will they be fooled again? I am afraid so. The people have always been amenable to oratory of this sort. The workers know they have no enemies except their masters. They know that their citizenship papers are no warrant for the safety of themselves or their wives and children. They know that honest sweat, persistent toil and years of struggle bring them nothing worth holding on to, worth fighting for. Yet, deep down in their foolish hearts they believe they have a country. Oh blind vanity of slaves!

The clever ones, up in the high places know how childish and silly the workers are. They know that if the government dresses them up in khaki and gives them a rifle and starts them off with a brass band and waving banners, they will go forth to fight valiantly for their own enemies. They are taught that brave men die for their country's honor. What a price to pay for an abstraction — the lives of millions of young men; other millions crippled and blinded for life; existence made hideous for still more millions of human beings; the achievement and inheritance of generations swept away in a moment — and nobody better off for all the misery! This terrible sacrifice would be comprehensible if the thing you die for and call country, fed, clothed, housed and warmed you, educated and cherished your children. I think the workers are the most unselfish of the children of men; they toil and live and die for other people's country, other people's sentiments, other people's liberties and other people's happiness! The workers have no liberties of their own; they are not free when they are compelled to work 12 or 10 or eight hours a day. They are not free when they are ill paid for their exhausting toil. They are not free when their children must labor in mines, mills and factories or starve, and when their women may be driven by poverty to lives of shame. They are not free when they are clubbed and imprisoned because they go on strike for a raise of wages and for the elemental justice that is their right as human beings.

We are not free unless the men who frame and execute the laws represent the interests of the lives of the people and no other interest. The ballot does not make a free man out of a wage slave. There has never existed a truly free and democratic nation in the world. From time immemorial men have followed with blind loyalty the strong men who had the power of money and of armies. Even while battlefields were piled high with their own dead they have tilled the lands of the rulers and have been robbed of the fruits of their labor. They have built palaces and pyramids, temples and cathedrals that held no real shrine of liberty.

As civilization has grown more complex the workers have become more and more enslaved, until today they are little more than parts of the machines they operate. Daily they face the dangers of railroad, bridge, skyscraper, freight train, stokehold, stockyard, lumber raft and mine. Panting and straining at the docks, on the railroads and underground and on the seas, they move the traffic and pass from land to land the precious commodities that make it possible for us to live. And what is their reward? A scanty wage, often poverty, rents, taxes, tributes and war indemnities.

The kind of preparedness the workers want is reorganization and reconstruction of their whole life, such as has never been attempted by statesmen or governments. The Germans found out years ago that they could not raise good soldiers in the slums so they abolished the slums. They saw to it that all the people had at least a few of the essentials of civilization — decent lodging, clean streets, wholesome if scanty food, proper medical care and proper safeguards for the workers in their occupations. That is only a small part of what should be done, but what wonders that one step toward the right sort of preparedness has wrought for Germany! For 18 months it has kept itself free from invasion while carrying on an extended war of conquest, and its armies are still pressing on with unabated vigor. It is your business to force these reforms on the administration. Let there be no more talk about what a government can or cannot do. All these things have been done by all the belligerent nations in the hurly-burly of war. Every fundamental industry has been managed better by the governments than by private corporations.

It is your duty to insist upon still more radical measures. It is your business to see that no child is employed in an industrial establishment or mine or store, and that no worker is needlessly exposed to accident or disease. It is your business to make them give you clean cities, free from smoke, dirt and congestion. It is your business to make them pay you a living wage. It is your business to see that this kind of preparedness is carried into every department of the nation, until every one has a chance to be wellborn, well nourished, rightly educated, intelligent and serviceable to the country at all times.

Strike against all ordinances and laws and institutions that continue the slaughter of peace and the butcheries of war. Strike against war, for without you no battles can be fought. Strike against manufacturing shrapnel and gas bombs and all other tools of murder. Strike against preparedness that means death and misery to millions of human beings. Be not dumb, obedient slaves in an army of destruction. Be heroes in an army of construction.

## The Ford Peace Plan is Doomed to Failure
New York *Call*, (1915)

Henry Ford belongs to the same class as the diplomats and politicians that made the war. Nothing will come of his plan, because he won't use the only means to make it a success —

get the soldiers themselves to quit fighting.

The Roman peace was a failure, the truce of God was only a truce, and the treaties of governments end in new wars. It is time to sweep aside these artificial peacemakers and declare the peace of man. If the soldiers in the trenches once understood that their victories belong to their governments, but their miseries are their own, they will cease to fight at the bidding of an officer backed by an official. They will put their hands in their pockets and go home. If the Kaiser and the Czar and a group of presidents and kings are interested in a quarrel about a line fence, the workers they have turned into soldiers will let them have their fight out among themselves.


# Menace of the Militarist Program
New York *Call* (1916)

The burden of war always falls heaviest on the toilers. They are taught that their masters can do no wrong, and go out in vast numbers to be killed on the battlefield. And what is their reward? If they escape death they come back to face heavy taxation and have their burden of poverty doubled. Through all the ages they have been robbed of the just rewards of their patriotism as they have been of the just reward of their labor.

The only moral virtue of war is that it compels the capitalist system to look itself in the face and admit it is a fraud. It compels the present society to admit that it has no morals it will not sacrifice for gain. During a war, the sanctity of a home, and even of private property is destroyed. Governments do what it is said the "crazy socialists" would do if in power.

In spite of the historical proof of the futility of war, the United States is preparing to raise a billion dollars and a million soldiers in preparation for war. Behind the active agitators for defense you will find J.P. Morgan & Co., and the capitalists who have invested their money in shrapnel plants, and others that turn out implements of murder. They want armaments because they beget war, for these capitalists want to develop new markets for their hideous traffic.

I look upon the whole world as my fatherland, and every war has to me the horror of a family feud. I look upon true patriotism as the brotherhood of man and the service of all to all. The only fighting that saves is the one that helps the world toward liberty, justice and an abundant life for all.

To prepare this nation in the true sense of the word, not for war, but for peace and happiness, the state should govern every department of industry, health and education in such a way as to maintain the bodies and minds of the people in soundness and efficiency. Then, the nation will be prepared to withstand the demand to fight for a perpetuation of its own slavery at the bidding of a tyrant.

After all, the best preparedness is one that disarms the hostility of other nations and makes friends of them. Nothing is to be gained by the workers from war. They suffer all the miseries, while the rulers reap the rewards. Their wages are not increased, nor their toil made lighter, nor their homes made more comfortable. The army they are supposed to raise can be used to break strikes as well as defend the people.

If the democratic measures of preparedness fall before the advance of a world empire, the worker has nothing to fear. No conqueror can beat down his wages more ruthlessly or oppress him more than his own fellow citizens of the capitalist world are doing. The worker has nothing to lose but his chains, and he has a world to win. He can win it at one stroke from a world empire. We must form a fully equipped, militant international union so that we can take possession of such a world empire.

This great republic is a mockery of freedom as long as you

are doomed to dig and sweat to earn a miserable living while the masters enjoy the fruit of your toil. What have you to fight for? National independence? That means the masters' independence. The laws that send you to jail when you demand better living conditions? The flag? Does it wave over a country where you are free and have a home, or does it rather symbolize a country that meets you with clenched fists when you strike for better wages and shorter hours? Will you fight for your masters' religion which teaches you to obey them even when they tell you to kill one another?

Why don't you make a junk heap of your masters' religion, his civilization, his kings and his customs that tend to reduce a man to a brute and God to a monster? Let there go forth a clarion call for liberty. Let the workers form one great worldwide union, and let there be a globe encircling revolt to gain for the workers true liberty and happiness.

# To Morris Hillquit
New York *Call*, (1917)

I have refrained from writing, or giving utterance to the fierce protest in my heart against the war madness that is sweeping away the reason and commonsense of our people, because I believed that President Wilson would defend our liberties and stay with his strong hand the forces that are invading them. I have waited and waited for some word from the White House. I have prayed and hoped against hope that today, tomorrow or next day the newspapers would contain a rebuke that would bring the nation back to sanity and tolerance. I have read and read President Wilson's own lofty utterance about freedom, justice and the rights of the people against the rights of governments. I thought he must realize that the Trading With the Enemy Act does not differ essentially from the drastic measure which the Federalists of 1798 rushed through Congress. In the quiet of his study he wrote that the Sedition Act cut perilously near the root of freedom of speech and of the press. He saw clearly that there was no telling where such power would stop. Who can tell where the power given by the Trading With the Enemy Act will stop an act that makes the Postmaster General absolute dictator over the press, an act that renders it impossible for any publication criticizing any measure of the government to circulate through the mails, be sent by express or freight, or sold...

Now you know, and the voters of New York know, when they are in their right minds, that it is neither treasonable nor seditious to criticize any statute or law. Nor is it treasonable to agitate for the repeal of any act. We are within our constitutional rights as citizens to agitate for the abolition of conscription. Why should we give up the best things we have, freedom of speech, of the press and of assemblage and establish kaiserism in this country while we send our armies to destroy it in Europe? I am not discussing the war, its causes, its origin, its righteousness or unrighteousness, or whether the Christian spirit is eternally opposed to it or not.

I am not opposed to war for sentimental reasons. The blood of fighting ancestors flows in my veins. I would gladly see our young men go forth to battle if I thought it was a battle for true freedom. I would gladly participate in a way that would really make the world safe for democracy. In making the world safe for democracy I do not mean simply to put down autocracy in Germany...

I do not know if your election would bring about a speedy peace. But I do know that it would encourage us to look forward to a people's peace — a peace without victory, a peace without conquests or indemnities. I would that a large vote cast for you would be a strong protest against the Prussian militarism that is taking possession of our government. It would be an unequivocal denial that New York City stands for the kind of democracy that prevails here just now; a democracy where freedom of assemblage is denied the people; a democracy where armed officials behave like thugs, forcibly dispersing meetings, burning literature and clubbing the people; a democracy where workingmen are arrested and imprisoned for exercising their right to strike; a democracy where the miners of Bisbee were torn from their homes, huddled in freight cars like cattle, flung upon a desert without food or water and left to die; a democracy where negroes may be massacred and their property burned, as was done in East St. Louis; a democracy where lynching and child labor are tolerated; a democracy where a minister who follows the feet of the Messenger of Peace — beautiful upon the earth — was flogged almost to death, and the only comment of the press upon this outrage was a series of facetious remarks and a half concealed approval of the "hotheaded Kentuckians whose earnestness and patriotism carried them a little too far."

If I had the right to vote, I would vote for you, Mr. Hillquit, because a vote for you would be a blow at the militarism that is one of the chief bulwarks of capitalism, and the day that militarism is undermined, capitalism will fall.

# To Eugene V. Debs
New York *Call* (1919)

Of course, the Supreme Court has sustained the decision of the lower court in your case. To my mind, the decision has added another laurel to your wreath of victories. Once more you are going to prison for upholding the liberties of the people.

I write because my heart cries out, and will not be still. I write because I want you to know that I should be proud if the Supreme Court convicted me of abhorring war, and doing all in my power to oppose it. When I think of the millions who have suffered in all the wicked wars of the past, I am shaken with the anguish of a great impatience. I want to fling myself against all brute powers that destroy life and break the spirit of man.

In the persecution of our comrades there is one satisfaction. Every trial of men like you, every sentence against them, tears away the veil that hides the face of the enemy. The discussion and agitation that follows the trials define, more sharply, the positions that must be taken before all men can live together in peace, happiness and security.

We were driven into the war for liberty, democracy and humanity. Behold what is happening all over the world today! Oh, where is the swift vengeance of Jehovah, that it does not fall upon the hosts of those who are marshalling machine guns against hunger stricken people? It is the complacency of madness to call such acts "preserving law and order." Law and order! What oceans of blood and tears are shed in their name! I have come to loathe traditions and institutions that take away the rights of the poor and protect the wicked against judgment.

The wise fools who sit in the high places of justice fail to see that, in revolutionary times like the present, vital issues are settled, not by statutes, decrees and authorities, but in spite of them. Like the Girondins in France, they imagine that force can check the onrush of revolution. Thus they sow the wind, and unto them shall be the harvest of the whirlwind.

You dear comrade! I have long loved you because you are an apostle of brotherhood and freedom. For years I have thought of you as a dauntless explorer going toward the dawn and, like a humble adventurer, I have followed in the trail of your footsteps. From time to time the greetings that have come back to me from you have made me very happy, and now I reach out my hand and clasp yours through prison bars.

With heartfelt greetings, and with a firm faith that the cause for which you are now martyred shall be all the stronger because of your sacrifice and devotion, I am,

Yours for the revolution. May it come swiftly, like a shaft sundering the dark!

# resources

## web resources

**American Foundation For The Blind**
www.afb.org
*Great resource including some rare material and images.*

**Helen Keller Reference Archive**
www.marxists.org
*Resource focusing on Keller's radicalism and socialist beliefs. Includes Keller's FBI file.*

## by Helen Keller

*Helen Keller: Her Socialist Years*, edited by Philip Foner, 1967

*Helen Keller's Journal,* 1938

*Peace at Eventide,* 1932

*Midstream: My Later Life,* 1930

*Light In My Darkness,* 1927

*Out Of The Dark,* 1913

*The Song Of The Stonewall,* 1910

*The World I Live In,* 1908

*Optimism, An Essay,* 1903

*Story of My Life,* 1903

## other writers

*Helen Keller: Rebellious Spirit,* by Laurie Lawlor, 2001

*Helen Keller: A Life,* by Dorothy Herrman, 1989

# rebel lives

## haydée santamaría
### *edited by Betsy Maclean*

"Haydée Santamaría signifies a world, an attitude, a sensibility as well as a revolution." – *Mario Benedetti*

Haydée first achieved notoriety by being one of two women who participated in the armed attack that sparked the Cuban Revolution. Later, as director of the world-renowned literary institution, Casa de las Americas, she embraced culture as a tool for social change and provided refuge for exiled Latin American artists and intellectuals.

**Includes reflections by Ariel Dorfman, Eduardo Galeano, Alicia Alonso, Silvio Rodríguez and Gabriél García Márquez.**

ISBN 1-876175-59-1 / US$11.95

## albert einstein
### *edited by Jim Green*

"What I like most about Albert Einstein is that he was a troublemaker." – Fred Jerome, author of *The Einstein File*

You don't have to be Einstein… to know that he was a giant in the world of science and physics. This book takes a new, subversive look at *Time* magazine's "Person of the Century," whose passionate opposition to war and racism and advocacy of human rights put him on the FBI's files as a socialist enemy of the state.

ISBN 1-876175-63-X / US$9.95

## oceanpress

e-mail info@oceanbooks.com.au
www.oceanbooks.com.au